NURTURING INTIMACY WITH GOD

Nurturing Intimacy with God

Pamela Hoover Heim

NELSON

THOMAS NELSON PUBLISHERS

Nashville

Library of Congress Cataloging-in-Publication Data

Heim, Pamela.
    Nurturing intimacy with God / Pamela Heim.
        p.   cm.
    ISBN 0-8407-3132-9
    1. Spiritual life.   2. Intimacy (Psychology)—Religious aspects—Christianity.   I. Title.
BV4501.2.H36945   1990
248.4—dc20   90-38625
                                                            CIP

            1 2 3 4 5 — 93 92 91 90

To

Raynee Daley,
her Abba's child.

ACKNOWLEDGEMENTS

My thanks go to some special people who have
made this book possible.

My husband, Lowell,
for his support and the gentle thumb he keeps
in my back;

the Broadmoor Bible Class
for asking me to teach them how to nurture
intimacy with God, thus, making me collect
my thoughts on the subject;

Ronald Haynes
for believing in my manuscript and taking it
to Thomas Nelson Publishers;

my editor, Susan Salmon,
for her cheerful, wise counsel.

CONTENTS

PART I   UNDERSTANDING INTIMACY

1   The Hunger for Intimacy   *3*
2   Discover Your Father   *14*
3   Find Your Husband   *26*
4   Receive the Gift   *37*

PART II   UNDERSTANDING GOD

5   Prevent Idolatry   *53*
6   Embrace the Word   *64*
7   Engage the Spirit   *74*

PART III   UNDERSTANDING MYSELF

8   Look Beyond Skin Deep   *89*
9   Get It Down in Writing   *101*

PART IV   INTEGRATING UNDERSTANDING

10   Think Things Through   *119*
11   Believe It's True   *132*
12   Prayer that Transforms   *143*

PART V   REALIZING UNDERSTANDING

13   Share the Love   *157*
14   Hurdle the Barriers   *169*

PART ONE

UNDERSTANDING

INTIMACY

I have put aside all else,
counting it worth less than nothing,
in order that I can have Christ,
and become one with him
(Phil. 3:8–9, LB).

CHAPTER 1

THE HUNGER FOR INTIMACY

I've heard people imply that true "spiritual giants" spend most of their waking moments in Bible reading or on their knees or faces in prayer. They witness door-to-door or preach on street corners. They live in monasteries or at least sell all they possess and take their place among the poor in the world's major urban areas. They probably spend weeks at a time in silent retreat. And they liberally sprinkle their conversation with God-talk and pious phrases. They work signs and wonders. They don't like food or sex, and they don't get the flu.

It's possible, however, for us Christians

to work more to get close to Christ and enjoy Him less and sense we are farther from Him. We can do what makes us look like Christians and still not experience the integrity of a Christian life. We may go through spiritual activities and yet not see the kind of change we would expect to see in ourselves if we truly were spending productive time in intimate fellowship with Christ; for all our strenuous effort we lament that we don't act much like Him. All of this is quite frustrating if we have thought of Scripture reading, prayer, fasting, giving, and other acts of devotion as buttons we push to get guaranteed spiritual results.

Intimacy, however, whether with God or with other people, is a matter of being in relationship rather than observing rules. I believe that what the body of Christ needs today is to be consumed less with duty and more with devotion, to try less and trust more, to engage in fewer works and more worship, to center less on policies and programs and more on passion.

I'm thrilled with what I observe as an increasing interest among many believers in the whole area of what has been called spirituality. Seminaries are offering courses in it; a student can even get a doctorate in the subject. (I took a course from one who had.) Books are coming out on spiritual disciplines; one authority identified almost fifty of these exercises which promote godliness.

But this book is not a call to develop reputed religious giants. It deals with principles rather than formulas. In considering intimacy with our Creator, it focuses on the keys to any quality relationship—mutual openness, knowledge, understanding, acceptance, love, and appreciation—and includes the means to discover and express those.

WHAT IS INTIMACY?

For more than twenty years, my friend and I laughed, cried, worked, and played together. Then because of circumstances, our paths separated. When she called one day to tell me she was coming for a visit, I was delighted. I couldn't wait to see her and catch up on the significant experiences we'd had since we'd last been together. I wanted to share with her my excitement about a project I had just completed for a Christian ministry to poor children.

A couple of days after she arrived, I eagerly sat her down to show her a thirty-minute video featuring three mothers I'd met in a barrio in Ecuador. I had spent a day with each woman, observing them as they cared for their children in split-bamboo homes and interviewing them about their fears and hopes for their families. Those three days had made a profound impact on me; I would never be quite the same again. I wanted my friend to understand something of my life-changing experience. It was kind of like wanting to introduce my old friend to my new ones.

I slipped the cassette into the VCR. The faces and voices of Esilda, Maria, and Lourdes, in many ways women like the two of us, filled the room. We saw three concerned mothers struggle against enormous odds to provide for their children's needs. We heard a challenge to do what we could to help make a difference for needy women and children in developing countries.

As the credits rolled, I turned off the machine. The television went black. I sat back down on the sofa and looked at my friend.

"You can hardly believe people live like that," she said. And then she changed the subject. She spoke of one thing and another, but she didn't mention my time in Guayaquil or the women I'd met there.

I felt . . . well, I'm not sure what all I felt. I know I was stunned. Chagrined. Hurt. Disappointed. Rejected. And lonely. Sadly, achingly lonely. I felt as if I hadn't connected with my friend, that she hadn't heard or understood me, like my efforts were unappreciated. Sitting with her in my family room, I felt soul-alone, shut out.

My feelings that day were not new to me, though I have been a loved child, successful student, college campus leader, happy wife, devoted mother, and productive professional woman. I've wondered from time to time, *How can anybody from a happy family be lonely? Is there something wrong with me? If my peers seem to like me, then why do I have times when I feel I don't fit in? If I'm loved and I know I am, then why do I sense I'm not really connecting with others in areas that are important to me? Why do I think nobody truly understands the real me?*

Perhaps you've felt this way. You've sensed a desperate longing at the core of your being, but you can't seem to satisfy it. It may have hit you when you were homesick to see family or friends, but when you finally got together with them, something was missing. Maybe it was when you were on vacation with your spouse, and you were hoping for a second honeymoon beyond your dreams. You anticipated that a time of getting away from demanding schedules and focusing on each other would help the two of you touch on a soul-to-soul level. And then you discovered that even a wonderful resort complete with sunny skies, palm trees, white beaches, and turquoise water wasn't enough to erase your sense of being a married single. You've been lonely. And you understand the feeling Walter Wangerin described as "a worm forever feeding in your vitals."[1]

I'm convinced that loneliness is endemic to human beings, and it thrives in epidemic proportions. I see it affecting all ages, all races, every nationality, both sexes, and folks at every economic level. Paul Tillich understood loneliness this way: "Being alive means being in a body . . . separated from all other bodies. And being separated means being alone. This is true of every creature, and . . . more true of man than any other creature. He is not only alone; he also *knows* that he is alone. . . . It is his destiny to be alone and to be aware of it."[2]

Aware of our loneliness, we desire deeply fulfilling relationships. We crave intimacy, a comfortable sense of being respected, emotionally supported, and cared for by a person we value. We want a walls-down-roof-off relationship. We long for somebody with whom to share our secrets and be vulnerable. We yearn to relate without self-protective defensiveness and stand soul-naked before each other, stripped of all that prevents our being seen and known but not abandoned when seen and known. We desire to be loved for who we are, regardless of what another discovers about us. *This intimacy we want is a close, loving, satisfying relationship which results from two persons' mutual self-disclosure, deep understanding, and appreciative acceptance of one another's essential and authentic selves.*

Sensing both our loneliness and our desire for intimacy, we are acutely disappointed when we experience the rejection and misunderstanding I did from my friend. We feel troubled when instead of getting what we want, we experience what Phyllis Hobe called "a thin curtain of individuality that keeps us apart." Thus, we sometimes go to great lengths to tear down that curtain.

THE FIGHT TO FIND THE FIX

We may seek to relieve our painful loneliness by stuffing the void we feel with family and friends and houses and cars and clothes. We may work hard, sometimes in fascinating jobs, to distract us from our relational poverty. We may use sex, baring our bodies, though we fear baring our souls, in hopes of establishing a satisfying bond with another. We may travel and dine out and attend concerts and visit galleries and play sports until we're exhausted with figuring out ways to plug our emptiness. We may spend enormous sums on recreation that often does nothing to re-create us or create a sense of belonging with others. Like junkies pursuing a fix, we may spend our lives looking for a permanent high through self-administered hits of power, possessions, diversions, or using people. But none of these can permanently satisfy us.

What we are intensely searching for is the intimate relationship we were created for—a relationship with God made possible through Jesus Christ. A loving, communicating Creator made us in His image to enjoy Him. He fashioned us to connect with Him on a deeply personal, fulfilling level. Our first parents experienced this perfect relationship when they lived with each other without sin in a world without sin.

We, however, don't live as Adam and Eve did before the Fall. Because sin has thrust its ugly head into our world and messed up every aspect of life on earth, we don't just automatically experience security and significance in a loving, trusting relationship with the Lord, even though He knows and cares about us and the most minute details of our lives.

Fashioned for intimacy with God, we are bound to feel lonely when we sense any separation from Him. Jesus described this as being like branches cut off from the life-source Vine: "If anyone does not remain in me, he is like a branch that is thrown away and withers" (John 15:6 NIV). So our goal is to get and stay connected to God so that, as the apostle Paul put it, for us to live is Christ. This means our spirits touch and link with His Spirit with the result that we know we are intimately bonded with Him and share in His life.

Falling short of this kind of intimacy with the Lord, we sometimes expect to find in fallible, finite people His unconditional love and infinite acceptance. Nobody, however, not even the most magnificent human being on this great earth, can be to us what He is. Still, we sometimes ask people to give us what only He can give us, and in the process, we frustrate ourselves and use them badly.

Mary Dixon Thayer noted, "Always there remain portions of our heart into which no one is able to enter, invite them as we may." People cannot pierce every area of our isolation and destroy it because they can't provide perfect love, total acceptance, and complete respect. Only God can. Only He can meet our deepest longing for intimacy because He knows and loves us and at the same time allows us to know Him in a deeply personal relationship.

The psalmist experienced this yearning for his Creator as a thirst: "As the deer pants for the water brooks, so pants my soul for You, O God. My soul thirsts for God, for the living God" (Psalm 42:1,2). When Jesus met the woman at the well, she was thirsty like that. Jesus knew that she craved something and that she had tried, but failed, to satisfy her craving in marriage to five men. He told her He could quench her thirst: "Whoever drinks of the water that I shall give him will never thirst. But the water that I shall give him will become in him a fountain of water welling up into everlasting life" (John 4:14).

Later Christ satisfied the physical hunger of the multitude with bread and fish, but He understood their spiritual hunger went deeper. He offered them the Bread that gives Life to the world. He declared, "I am the bread of life. He who comes to Me shall never hunger, and he who believes in Me shall never thirst" (John 6:35). At the supper on the night before His crucifixion, He likened His blood and body to wine and bread and told His disciples to drink and eat Him, to assimilate His life into their very own.

To have life is to live in relationship to the One who said, "I am Living Water. I am the Bread of Life. I am Life." Our greatest hunger is for the Bread of Life; our primary thirst is for the Living Water; our ultimate need is His life. That's why He encouraged us to live intimately bonded with Him in order to satiate and quench our soul-craving. Because of this, I believe loneliness, our spiritual hunger and thirst, is to intimacy with God what physical hunger is to eating and physical thirst is to drinking. It is the impetus which prompts us to move toward Him. We will experience wholeness only to the extent that we seek and find a delightful, restful, satisfying connection with Jesus Christ.

The following pages are addressed to garden-variety believers who desire a closer relationship with the Lord, not to an elite sort of Christian who has the resources and inclination to detach from normal life to pursue a hothouse spirituality. It is for people who want to work for a living and enjoy spending time with friends. It's for folks who deal with spouses and children and parents and co-workers. It's for singles struggling with dating or the lack of it and married couples who make love enthusiastically. It's for women and men who like to eat and sleep, who conscientiously carve dandelions out of their lawns when necessary, and who have to take out the garbage.

In spite of its simplicity, I don't think you'll find the following trivial. It calls you and me to nurture intimacy with God, to make a passionate commitment to understand and experience truth in such a way that our lives are changed because the real you and I have connected with the real God.

CHAPTER 2

DISCOVER YOUR FATHER

What does a solid, satisfying relationship with the Lord look like? The Bible gives us several examples of how the Creator interacts with His creation, in general, and His followers, in particular. But the two primary ones come from the home. God invites us to have the loving, intimate relationship with Him that exists between a good parent and a child and between a loving husband and his wife.

Twisted human models of these relationships, however, tend to warp our understanding of the intimacy that is to be the norm between God and us. I think of a lovely young woman who came to talk to me at a retreat at which I was speaking. She told me she had a difficult time trusting and loving her heavenly Father. I understood why when I learned that her earthly father had sexually abused her throughout most of her growing up years. If God was anything like her father, how could she possibly believe God cared for and protected her?

God's object lessons do get warped by the disintegration of family relationships in our society. Divorce, spouse battering (both physical and verbal), child abuse, rejection, neglect, and emotional detachment have caused pain and wreaked devastation for millions in our country. And as terrible as the normal consequences of these problems are on individuals and community life, equally horrendous is the distortion of God's primary illustrations of who He is.

Since the Lord calls Himself a parent, our perception of the relationship between us and our parents is important. No matter how young or old we are, we seem to crave a satisfying relationship with our father and mother. Even we middle-aged people feel a sense of frustration and loss if we have never experienced adequate love and acceptance from one or both of our parents. Dr. Harold Bloomfield notes, "No one seems to be immune to the complex and harmful effects of unresolved conflict with one's parents. . . . Having conflicting and unresolved feelings about them can affect your moment-to-moment health and well-being, your satisfaction with your career, work and leisure time, and your most significant emotional relationships."[1]

That includes our relationship with God. How we feel about our parents often has a direct bearing on our willingness to nurture intimacy with the Lord. That's why some folks who have seen a poor excuse of a parent in their earthly dads and moms can hardly tolerate the idea of God as a parent. But even they seem to know what a good father or mother is like, despite their negative experience. They seem to have some standard against which they judge how well a parent functions.

We are working backwards, however, if we make comparisons by starting with our parents and ending up with our heavenly Father. We need to begin with Him. He is the essential standard against which we measure all parents, not vice versa, because even the most outstanding human parent is a greatly limited imitation of God. So when we call Him our parent, we are saying He's like the best mother or father we can imagine—and still far superior to that.

(Some folks have experienced such abuse or neglect that they would probably benefit from counseling in order to help them deal with the wounds of their childhood, feelings which may affect their ability to relate to God and to others. My observation is that few women, for example, can work through the long-lasting impact of in-

cest without the support of a wise friend or counselor. Even the most consistent and fervent prayers may not be able to pray the putrefaction of
that sore out of their lives by themselves.)

A PICTURE OF ABBA

Jesus especially revealed God as our parent. In the Old Testament, as Hannah Whitall
Smith wrote, "God was not revealed as the Father
so much as a great warrior fighting for His people,
or as a mighty king ruling over them and caring
for them. The name of Father is only given to
Him a very few times there, six or seven at the
most."[2]

That doesn't mean that God didn't act
toward His people as a Father to His children.
We see His generous provision for Abraham,
Isaac, Jacob, and their descendants. He called the
Israelites "a special treasure to Me" (Ex. 19:5).
He gave them a homeland. He protected and
rescued them even when they got themselves
into trouble through their own wrongdoing. He
treated them with patience and kindness when
they surely deserved His anger and punishment.
He gave them second, third, and more chances;
He kept hanging in there with them. He revealed
Himself as being full of forgiveness, mercy, and
grace. He gave ample evidence that He is a God
who is like the best of parents.

Still, the Old Testament people of God

did not address Him as Father. In fact, they probably couldn't conceive of doing so since they were extremely careful about even saying or writing His name, Yahweh. Calling Him Abba, the Aramaic word for Daddy, would have been unthinkable, even sacrilege, to them. So, when Jesus came on the scene, we find the Jewish leaders feared God, tried to please Him through keeping countless rules, and believed He would rather a person be crippled than healed on the Sabbath. They called Abraham their father, but they didn't call their Creator that.

Yet in the New Testament, the primary means of referring to the first person of the Trinity is by the word *Father*. When His followers asked Him to teach them to pray, Jesus said, "When you pray say: Father" (Luke 11:1,2). His Sermon on the Mount made repeated references to the Father in heaven whom they should praise, address in prayer, trust, and expect good gifts and rewards from.[3]

Perhaps the most poignant illustration of God's parenting is found in the story Jesus told of the man who had two sons. The younger asked for his inheritance early, promptly split from his family, and blew his money in an orgy of self-indulgence. When he came to the end of his rope, he decided to return to his father and ask simply for a menial position in the family business. While he was on the road to his home, his father spotted him, *ran* to greet him, gave him a bear hug, and kissed him (Luke 15:11–20). I've heard that a Chinese artist painted this story showing the running father shod in mismatched shoes, kicking up the dust as he went. He was so eager to reach his child that he had stuffed his feet into the first sandals he could find. Jesus said that is the kind of father we have in God.

How unlike most earthly parents is that picture Jesus painted of our Father. He didn't wait to show love. Wait for the child to knock on the door. Wait for the right words of remorse from the prodigal. Wait for proof that the kid had turned over a new leaf. Wait to embrace and give gifts. He was extravagant in both his pardon and affection, so much so that the prodigal's older brother got angry at his dad's generosity to the wayward son. The "good" son was like the Pharisees, who saw a God primarily concerned with law, order, and justice rather than a Father of grace, forgiveness, and love.

Yet Smith reminded us that the Fatherhood of God underscores all that He is to us: "This name [Father] must underlie every other name by which He has ever been known. Has He been called a Judge? Yes, but He is a Father Judge, one who judges as a loving father would. Is He a King? Yes, but He is a King who is at the same time the Father of His subjects and who rules them with a father's tenderness. Is He a Lawgiver? Yes, but He is a Lawgiver who gives laws as a father would, remembering the weakness and ignorance of his helpless children."[4]

You and I have the high privilege of relating to our Judge, King, and Lawgiver as our loving Parent. How do we do that? We begin by accepting Jesus Christ as our Savior: "As many as received Him, to them He gave the right to become children of God, even to those who believe in His name: who were born, not of blood, nor of the will of the flesh, nor of the will of man, but of God" (John 1:12,13). The intimacy of the family is for those who have been born anew into His Family by the Spirit of God. Those who have experienced spiritual birth know God as their heavenly Father.

By the Spirit, it is our privilege as dependent children to cry, " 'Abba, Father.' The Spirit Himself bears witness with our spirit that we are children of God, and if children, then heirs—heirs of God and joint heirs with Christ" (Rom. 8:15–17).

God wants everybody everywhere to come to repentance and become His children and heirs of His spiritual riches (2 Pet. 3:9). That, however, doesn't mean we have no choice in the matter of our membership in His family. We can choose whether or not we want to treat Him as our Father.

THE CHILD'S CHOICE

Hosea gives us a glimpse of what it's like for God when people decide to reject Him:

> When Israel was a child, I loved him, and out of Egypt I called my son. But the more I called Israel, the further they went from me. They sacrificed to the Baals and they burned incense to images. It was I who taught Ephraim to walk, taking them by the arms; but they did not realize it was I who healed them. . . . My people are determined to turn from me. . . . How can I give you up, Ephraim? How can I hand you over, Israel? How can I treat you like Admah? How can I make you like Zeboiim? My heart is changed within me; all my compassion is aroused (11:1–3,7,8,NIV).

(Admah and Zeboiim were peoples who suffered as a result of evil living.)

Can you feel the Father's grief? He's like the parent who, remembering the child as a sweet baby and a delightful toddler, is heartbroken at the adolescent's rebellion. He had wisely, tenderly done everything needed to raise a loving, respectful child, but the child repudiated him. And so Jeremiah 3:19 records the rejected Father saying, " 'How gladly would I treat you like sons and give you a desirable land, the most beautiful inheritance of any nation.' I thought you would call me 'Father' and not turn from following me" (NIV). But turn they did.

Jesus, like a bereft mother hen, felt that same spurning by His people: "O Jerusalem, Jerusalem, the one who kills the prophets and stones those who are sent to her! How often I wanted to gather your children together, as a hen gathers her chicks under her wings, but you were not willing!" (Matt. 23:37). Notice that Jesus was lamenting His children's rebellion. He was not breathing out threats. He wasn't plotting a way to punish or get even with those who defied or ignored Him.

Perhaps only we parents who have loved deeply, lavished kindness, hoped fervently, but nevertheless experienced rejection can understand the gut-wrenching agony of the heavenly Father. Though some theologians have been reluctant to acknowledge God's ability to suffer, the passages we have just read carry absolutely no weight if the Speaker did not intensely feel the hurt of the rejection He described. God grieves when we refuse His rightful place in our lives. At the same time, He is touched with the feeling of our weaknesses; He is sympathetic to our temptations and struggles when it comes to trusting and following Him (Heb. 4:15).

But how unthinkable that we should distance ourselves from the good Abba the Scripture shows Him to be: He loves us unconditionally, just as we are right now. He won't—can't—love us more tomorrow than He does today because today His love for us is like all His attributes, timeless and perfect and immutable and infinite. He never abandons us; He'll never, never leave us. He is wise, strong, and consistent yesterday, today, and forever.

He doesn't give us everything we ask for but all that we need, so we don't need to be anxious. He comforts us in our distress, but He doesn't allow us to be weaklings by making life easy for us. He disciplines us for our good. He encourages us to keep going when we feel like giving up. He is patient beyond imagination.

He holds us accountable to be our best. He doesn't allow us to be tempted beyond what we can bear; but when we blow it, He forgives us and then forgets our wrongdoings. He never expects more of us than we are capable of doing. What He asks us to do, He enables us to do; we are never without adequate resources. He counsels us about the way we should go and then walks that path with us. He gives us eternal life and the assurance that even death cannot separate us from Him.

And what does our loving Father expect from His children in return? I think of my own expectations as a mother. To be a good parent has been one of the driving forces of my life for the last twenty years. I have tried by God's enabling to be a reflection to my children of the kind of parent God is. And what have I wanted from them in return? Not fear or dutiful obedience or formal manners or the mindless compliance of rigid robots. All I have really desired is their love and a trust I've earned.

And that's what Jesus said the Father wants from us. When a ruler came to Him to ask which commandment was the most important one to obey, He answered, "You shall love the Lord your God with all your heart, with all your soul, with all your mind, and with all your strength" (Mark 12:28–30). That says to me that our heavenly Father wants from us what I want from my children: love and trust. But what about obedience? Where does that come in?

I've discovered in my relationship both with my children and with God that obedience comes easily when they love and trust me, when I love and trust Him. My son went through the normal adolescent process of growing in independence from Lowell and me. He did some healthy questioning of our values and beliefs, and he found he couldn't accept as his own everything we had taught or modeled for him. Because of his love and respect for us, however, he was never a rebellious teen. He told us he behaved at times as he knew we wanted him to just because he loved and honored us. In the final analysis, it was the love relationship, not rules, that protected him.

On the other hand, our adopted daughter came to us greatly damaged in her ability to love and trust. We quickly discovered that this inability meant that she could not obey from the heart, even when she did what we asked of her. Her compliance often seemed motivated more by a sense of ought to or have to, rather than want to. She reminded me of the cartoon kid who said, "I may be sitting down on the outside because you told me to, but I'm standing up on the inside."

Our heavenly Parent wants our obedience, the kind that comes from our loving Him enough to let His Holy Spirit work within us, helping us to want to obey Him and then helping us to do what He wants us to do (Phil. 2:13). He gives us both the desire and the ability to do His will so that our inner and outer selves are congruent—what we're doing on the outside comes from the inside—so that our actions are a deeply loving response to our heavenly Father, who loves us unfathomably more than the best earthly parents ever could.

CHAPTER 3

FIND
YOUR
HUSBAND

*T*he analogy of marriage adds vital dimensions to our concept of intimacy with the Lord, dimensions we don't find in the relationship between parent and child. Though the ties binding parents and children are strong, they are less intimate than those connecting a wife and husband. The Creator decreed this: "Therefore a man shall leave his father and mother and be joined to his wife" (Gen. 2:24).

God describes His relationship to His people as a marriage. It was Isaiah, the prophet, who explained that "Your Maker is your husband, the Lord of hosts is His name" (54:5).

God is a Husband to all believers; both males and females are to see themselves as His bride. In the New Testament the Son of God also likened Himself to a groom: When "John's disciples came and asked him, 'How is it that we and the Pharisees fast, but your disciples do not fast?' Jesus answered, 'How can the guests of the bridegroom mourn while he is with them?' " (Matt. 9:14,15).

It goes without saying that our heavenly Bridegroom offers a relationship that is totally opposite of the twisted marital relationships we may have experienced or know of—models characterized by distance, lack of communication, dominance, selfishness, thoughtlessness, cruelty, or infidelity. The foundation of our marriage with Christ is, in a word, love.

Our Bridegroom loves us with an everlasting love, and He rejoices over us, His bride (Jer. 31:3, Isa. 62:5). He wants to provide for us, to supply everything we need, to shower us with good and perfect gifts beyond all that we could ask or even think. He promises us His protection and care. He offers His wise counsel about the way we should go, but He doesn't nag or force His will on us.

He holds our hand as we walk through tough circumstances and comforts us in our sorrow; He's gentle with us in our frailty. He doesn't belittle us for being weak and human or crush us with condemnation. He's highly involved with us and never detaches Himself. No matter when we approach Him, He's not too busy to listen to us. He doesn't get tired of hearing us; therefore, if we want, we can talk all through the night to Him and He won't go to sleep on us. He doesn't clam up but freely expresses His loving thoughts toward us and openly shares His heart.

He always understands us. He loves us even when we fail Him and forgives us without making us grovel or do penance. He is totally trustworthy and can't be unfaithful to us. He will never abandon or divorce us. He is a perfect Spouse.

What He wants in return is that we relate to Him as a loving wife responds to her husband. Indeed we can learn much about what intimacy with God looks like by comparing it to marriage.

A PICTURE OF MARRIAGE

Marriage begins with a wedding. At a particular time, though perhaps we can't pinpoint it, we believers chose to enter into a covenant relationship with God. Maybe we'd spent time courting the idea about linking ourselves with Him. Then the day came when we knew we wanted personally and decisively to join our lives to Him. We wanted to belong to Him and receive Him as our own. Thus, we launched a new adventure as the bride of Christ.

Another comparison involves the fact that marriage initiates a separation. A man and woman detach themselves from their parents to live together in holy matrimony until death parts them. That happened for me in 1963 when Lowell and I spoke our vows to each other in a small Pennsylvania church one muggy August afternoon. At the outset, we understood from Scripture that our marriage bond was to take precedence over the parental one.

Paul spoke of us believers as having been bound to sin and the law and compelled to live under their dictates, but Christ freed us to experience the most profound separation from the law and sin because we died to them in Him. Reckoning ourselves dead releases us to be married to Christ and serve Him by means of the indwelling Holy Spirit (Rom. 7).

A third way our spiritual union with Christ compares to marriage has to do with the process of two becoming one. Lowell and I understood that we were to become one in our marriage; that was obvious from Scripture. We just weren't quite sure which one! We discovered it wasn't easy for either of us two self-centered and self-willed people to submit our individual wants for the good of our coupleness. Through the years, however, we struggled, learned, stretched, and grew enough to give up a great deal of our I-ness and you-ness in order to pursue our we-ness.

In the spiritual realm, you and I don't usually ask the overt question about whose will is paramount. We know who is to submit to Whom. We understand that to receive Jesus

Christ as Lord as well as Savior means that we choose to conform to His good and perfect will for our lives because He lovingly wills the best for us. In following His direction, we learn what it means to experience the oneness Jesus spoke of: "My prayer is . . . that all of them [believers] may be one, Father, just as you are in me and I am in you. May they also be in us. . . . I in them and you in me" (John 17:20–23, NIV).

To grow in oneness in marriage involves getting to know one another. Brides and grooms have a lot they don't understand about each other on their wedding day, things they discover only as time piles up.

That certainly has been true in my marriage. I like the way Scripture talks about sexual intercourse as knowing: "And Adam knew Eve his wife" (Gen. 4:1). Sexually, Lowell is the only man I've ever "known." Indeed, physical intimacy is knowing a person at a profoundly fundamental level. But in addition to this, I've learned dozens of things about Lowell that nobody else has—probably they wouldn't care to—because we've shared experiences, thoughts, dreams, and feelings with great openness for more than twenty-seven years now.

When we think of our heavenly Bridegroom, we understand that He knows us perfectly. He has a complete grasp of who we are, how we think and react, what motivates us, and what we need; we don't begin to know ourselves as well as He knows us. By contrast, we can spend a lifetime getting to know Him and never comprehend everything about Him. Every time we learn more about the Lover of our souls, we discover so much more to be explored and more reason to trust Him.

The longer we pursue intimate knowledge of Christ, the more we discover how perfect He is, that He is far beyond all that we could ever want. He is more than enough to meet the most intense longings of our souls. He is better than the best husband we can imagine. He is attractive in every way; He is altogether lovely.

By comparison, as we are naked before Him, we perhaps feel like elderly newlyweds, wishing we were more handsome or beautiful and had fewer wrinkles and less sagging. We want to stand before our Bridegroom with less sin in our past, without the scars of damaging choices, with more to recommend us, with some goodness that merits His love. But, "The Bridegroom . . . does not find, but makes her [His bride], lovely," as C. S. Lewis noted.[1] He makes us "holy, and blameless, and irreproachable" (Col. 1:22). Our Husband credits the bankrupt bride's account with all the righteousness of Christ so that she—we—can become holy as He is holy (Rom. 4:24).

A FAITHFUL HUSBAND

We will never feel that we love our heavenly Lover as He deserves, but that need not make us feel perpetually guilty and unhappy in the relationship. That's because any sense of discomfort we have in His splendid presence is eased by the look of love we see in His eyes and by the forgiving acceptance He offers without limit. Because we trust the love He has for us, *just the way we are,* we approach Him confidently and joyfully (Heb. 4:16).

We simply give Him our love, a reciprocal expression of our delight in the relationship. We draw near Him, appreciate Him, gladly release anything that causes dissonance in our harmony with Him, and believe that all else is well lost for the sake of knowing Him. Just as a couple may love each other as intensely in a restaurant as in a bedroom, our heavenly Husband wants us to love Him as much Monday through Saturday as we do on Sunday, as much on the highway and at home as we do at church. He desires that we speak well of Him in public in much the same way sweethearts can't seem to help talking about one another's good qualities to others.

He also wants us to meet Him regularly in a private place for the purpose of expressing our love to Him more intensely and personally than we can when people are around. He desires that we be vulnerable before Him, that we come into His presence without inhibition or holding anything back from Him. He delights in our eager impatience for that day when we'll be face to face with Him, without any sin, sorrow, or sickness impinging on the bliss of our union.

Our Husband asks us to trust Him and be faithful to Him. He hurts when we lust for other gods and idols as did His ancient people who committed what He called spiritual adultery: "Like a woman unfaithful to her husband, so you have been unfaithful to me" (Jer. 3:20, NIV).

Feel the betrayed Husband's pain when He said to Israel, "I remember the devotion of your youth, how as a bride you loved me and followed me through the desert. . . . Long ago you broke off your yoke and tore off your bonds; you said, 'I will not serve you!' Indeed, on every high hill and under every spreading tree you lay down as a prostitute. . . . How can you say, 'I am not defiled; I have not run after the Baals?' See how you behaved in the valley; consider what you have done. You are a swift she-camel running here and there, a wild donkey accustomed to the desert, sniffing the wind in her craving—in her heat who can restrain her?" (Jer. 2:2, 20–24, NIV).

Perhaps an even more wrenching passage is Ezekiel 16:6ff. In great detail the Lord describes His intricate involvement with Israel. He tells how He covered her in costly clothing and adorned her with precious jewels. He gave her expensive perfumes and provided her with gourmet foods. "Your fame went out among the nations because of your beauty, for it was perfect through My splendor which I had bestowed on you" (16:14).

No wonder the jilted Lover experienced

such anguish! "But you trusted in your own beauty, played the harlot because of your fame, and poured out your harlotry on everyone passing by who would have it" (16:15). The wife offered her precious God-given gifts to every sleazy satisfier of her appetites. She even offered her children, God's own creation, as a sacrifice to her god's greed.

And how did the Lord respond? Hosea reveals how the Husband, in the face of the infidelity of Israel, sought her as she plied her wicked trade, bought her, and restored her to His home. His indeed is a "love that wilt not let me go."

The truth is that all of us who are married to Christ have hurt Him in this way from time to time; we have been unfaithful. Perhaps we haven't been so overt in our infidelity as were those ancient people of God. Maybe, though, we've engaged in affairs of the heart. We've let our minds play with sinful attitudes and considered the possibility of dallying with some sinful act. Maybe we've allowed other things and people to take precedence over Him, determining to have who or what we want regardless of how that affected our relationship with Him. We've used a headache, tiredness, busyness, or some other flimsy excuse to rationalize our lack of nurturing intimacy with Him.

What causes adultery? I don't think spouses stray because they're ignorant of the rules; people know that they are to forsake all others and be true to their marriage partners. Most of the time unfaithfulness springs from a dissatisfaction with the marriage.

By the same token, I suspect that lack of acquaintance with God's law isn't at the root of spiritual adultery. I believe most of our unfaithfulness to our Bridegroom is because we've never gotten to know Him well enough to realize just how splendid He is, otherwise we'd have fallen irrevocably in love with Him. If we knew Him better, we would understand how safe we are to trust Him with our temptations, successes and failures, doubts, joys and sorrows, fears, love and anger, guilt, or whatever. We wouldn't try to hide from Him as if He were some punitive bully who feels threatened by our weaknesses. We couldn't find anybody or anything else more attractive than Him. But in our ignorance and perhaps distrust, we've become unenthusiastic, apathetic, or unfaithful lovers of Jesus Christ.

In spite of our infidelity, our Bridegroom remains faithful: "If we are faithless, He remains faithful; He cannot deny Himself" (2 Tim. 2:13). He never ceases to love and care for us. When we stray, He longs for us to return to His arms. Right at this minute, He's preparing a home to receive us, His bride, where He and we can live together in love for all eternity.

John saw all this in his vision of those days and recorded it in Revelation 19:6–8:

And I heard, as it were, the voice of a great multitude, as the sound of many waters and as the sound of mighty thunderings, saying, "Alleluia! For the Lord God Omnipotent reigns! Let us be glad and rejoice and give Him glory, for the marriage of the Lamb has come, and His wife has made herself ready." And to her it was granted to be arrayed in fine linen, clean and bright, for the fine linen is the righteous acts of the saints.

I can't begin to imagine the joy of that celebration of Love! However, the longer and better I've known God, the more I love Him. So I anticipate that joining Jesus Christ in heaven for that great feast will be joy unspeakable and full of glory.

The marriage supper of the Lamb should be simply another event in the lifelong earthly celebration of the union you and I have with Him—we've just changed the venue from earth to heaven. Until we make that move, the Bridegroom wants us to delight in our intimacy with Him in the here and now.

CHAPTER 4

RECEIVE THE GIFT

When we begin the venture of nurturing intimacy with God, we must understand that our relationship with Him, from start to finish, is a matter of grace. We don't deserve intimacy; we don't merit it; we simply accept it. "There is nothing we can do to earn this intimacy. It is God's gift to humanity in Jesus Christ, a gift that has already been given. . . . [A]ny deepening of intimacy with God depends entirely on God's grace and on his initiative," wrote Kenneth Swanson.[1]

The Bible clearly states that salvation is by grace alone (Eph. 2:8–9). And most of us

Christians readily assent to the principle that we can do nothing on our own to gain redemption. Instead we are redeemed because of the sacrifice of the Son of God. We readily echo Paul's reply to the jailer's question: "Believe on the Lord Jesus Christ, and you will be saved" (Acts 16:31). On the basis of faith alone, we say, our sins are forgiven; we are Abba's child; we will go to heaven to be with our Bridegroom when we die or when He returns for us.

The way some of us live, however, suggests that we consider future salvation the only gift we've received from our heavenly Father. We act as if, while we're left on earth, all our spiritual growth is a result of work, work, and more work. We know we become children of God by faith, but we live as if keeping membership in His family is a matter of sheer determination and effort. I did this for the first twenty years of my spiritual life.

I grew up in a church that defined a rigid code of conduct for Christians. Our lifestyle wasn't as confining as the Amish who lived nearby, but it was pretty narrow. I knew I was supposed to read my Bible, pray, go to all church services (four on Sunday, one mid-week, and any conferences that came along), witness to my faith, perform acts of service, and much more. On the negative side, I was not to smoke, drink, dance, wear make-up or earrings, or go to the movies or the county fair.

Being sincere about my faith from the time I committed my life to Christ as a preschooler, I diligently tried to comply with all the standards. And the truth is, I handled the rules very well. I had grown up with them; they were a part of my culture.

In spite of this, I was always a little on guard and off balance in my relationship with the One who called Himself my heavenly Father. I perpetually wondered, Was I doing enough or well enough? How would I know for sure? I identify with Joni Eareckson Tada, who likens a believer's trying to capture and keep God's attention to a high school girl who works pathetically hard to impress the guy on whom she has a crush.[2]

Then one day I finally began to comprehend just a little of what God's love is like. I had been to many deeper life conferences and graduated from an excellent church college at which I studied Bible and theology, but somehow I never grasped that my Father's love is not based on my performance. Then one day a campus minister sat at the dining room table of our parsonage. He told me that God loves me just the way I am today, that He'll never love me any less or any more no matter how much I grow in faith. He told me my Father would never disown me. He pointed out that His infinite capacity to forgive is more than enough to cover all my sins, and it is given freely without my begging and pleading with God for it. I'd never heard anything so heady, thrilling, encouraging, and comforting than the news that nothing could or would ever separate me from the Lord (Rom. 8:35–39). I decided to stake my life on the truth that I had come into a relationship with God by grace, and I couldn't develop it by works.

J. I. Packer explained well what I discovered: "Knowing God is a matter of *grace*. It is a relationship in which the initiative throughout is with God. . . . *We* do not make friends with *God; God* makes friends with *us*."[3]

THE PERFORMANCE TRAP

As I've observed people and read many spiritual biographies, however, I get the feeling that most Christians spend a part, if not all, of their spiritual lives trying to work their way into divine favor or earn a degree of closeness to God. Some of the Christians I've met in books adopted an ascetic lifestyle or withdrew to monasteries to devote their waking hours to meditation and centering on God. Some of the contemplative types equated "devotion with brooding over Christ's bodily sufferings, it . . . made them morbid about the spiritual value of physical pain."[4] So, some of them even engaged in self-torture and mutilation. These obviously zealous people were probably trying to develop, if not establish, their relationship with God.

Most of us have not gone to those lengths to enter or enhance a relationship with God. We may have, however, fallen into a performance trap; that is, we may believe that our relationship with Christ depends on how well we obey His rules.

David Seamands says the problem is that "many Christians have a sound biblical doctrine of grace to which they give full mental assent. It is a truth they *believe about* God, but it is not their gut-level basis of *living with* God. . . . It is *doctrinal* but not *relational;* it is believed *in* but not lived *out.*"[5]

Though we may have correct information in our heads that salvation is by grace through faith, our hearts may tell us that Bible study, prayer, giving, fellowship with other believers, fasting, corporate worship, service, and other spiritual activities are the key to gain or maintain God's favor and presence. We keep hoping that we can learn which works to perform or disciplines to observe that will help us develop our relationship with God in a way that feels good to us.

I don't especially like the term spiritual disciplines. That term can imply trying instead of trusting. Interestingly, the plural word disciplines is not in the Bible. The word *discipline,* which is in Scripture, comes from a Greek word that literally means "saving the mind." Sometimes the word is translated self-discipline.[6] If we use words like discipline and self-control, we need to understand that the source of these virtues is God and not self. They result from believing Him and not simply performing more in our own efforts. I think we sometimes confuse cause and effect: The relationship is the cause of our spiritual growth and activities.

THE FAITH FACTOR

Understand that I'm not suggesting that we're called to passivity, to sit like a lump on a lizard and just hope intimacy with our Father grows. When I say we must accept the gift, I mean we actively respond to truth. Hannah Whitall Smith said it succinctly, "Man's part is to trust, and God's part is to work."[7] If we aren't changing, then we're not trusting in the dynamic sense that the Bible uses the word.

When we continually place our faith in our Abba, He works in us so that we "may be partakers of the divine nature, having escaped the corruption that is in the world through lust" (2 Pet. 1:4). In other words, He changes us into the kind of people who can live devotedly and productively in His family. He progressively removes the sin that tarnishes our relationship and prevents intimacy with Him. (See chapter 11 for more on the matter of faith.)

We actively trust that God is at work in us, helping us want to obey Him and helping us do what He wants us to do (Phil. 2:13). This means He operates in the area of our wills. He not only enables us to do what pleases Him, He creates in us pure motivation to draw near to Him. That's important since our reasons for wanting intimacy with Him may be defective, making intimacy impossible.

SORT THROUGH THE MOTIVES

You and I may pursue our relationship with the Lord out of a sense of duty and its accompanying fear and guilt. These are miserable motivators in any relationship. They may work for a time, but they always take a toll somewhere. A relationship inevitably suffers when fear and guilt drive a scrupulous sense of duty. Not only does love cast out fear, as 1 John 4:18 says, but conversely, guilt and its accompanying fear ultimately will drive love away.[8]

No wonder guilt-, fear- and duty-motivated Christians often feel spiritually defeated and weak and don't experience much joy and satisfaction with their Father. If they were to admit it and if they were considering only the here-and-now and not eternity, they might say their relationship with God seems pretty one-sided ("I'm giving more than I'm getting"). If they were honest, they might say, "If I knew when I'd die, I'd wait to get right with God just before it happened." That's because we can't tolerate for very long the frustration of not living up to another's expectations, whether real or imagined. For that reason, I'm astonished that some folks unrelentingly walk the path of spiritual duty and somehow expect it to develop into a sense of intimacy with God.

The Christian life is meant to be a love relationship with our heavenly Father, our Friend, our Bridegroom—not an obligation. Love just doesn't speak in terms of duty: "I've *got* to phone my fiancee today" or "I *must* send her some flowers." John Piper wrote that his wife wouldn't feel too good about it if he took her out to dinner on their anniversary because he felt he owed it to her: "Neither God nor my wife is honored when we celebrate the high days of our relationship out of a sense of duty. They are honored when I delight in them."[9]

Another motivation for nurturing intimacy with God may be to escape reality, to use God as the ultimate pain-killer. We dare not, however, see drawing close to Him as a way of gaining leverage with Him so that He'll make life neat and sweet. Intimacy doesn't ensure obtaining an ecstasy that permits us to escape the reality of living in a fallen world.

Let me be honest. As long as the devil is running loose, this planet will never be heaven or even closely approximate it no matter how near we get to Christ. 'Tis *not* "heaven below my Redeemer to know." Joy, yes. Heaven, no.

We can experience love, joy, and peace here on earth, but we'll enjoy them along with suffering the discomforts of a world with a bad case of sin-sickness (John 16:33).

God's intimates, in both Old and New Testaments, were not "carried to the skies on flow'ry beds of ease." Not Abraham or Moses or David or the prophets or Mary or Jesus or Paul. It's unwarranted and unrealistic to assume that intimacy with God put the great saints on an emotional high that somehow lifted them above their physical, mental, and emotional torments in such a way that they hardly even felt them. So, we can't equate intimacy and ecstasy. Walking close to the Lord will not necessarily result in giddy good feelings which enable us to escape life's painful realities.

That's good news because feelings are notoriously fickle, and our best relationships can't depend on them. I relish feeling warm, fuzzy happiness in my marriage, but I also know the joy of quiet confidence that Lowell and I are bound in a love that enables us to walk in stable, satisfying understanding with one another when our emotions are flat. In the same way, intimacy with God has to do primarily with the relational, not the emotional. This doesn't mean that we won't occasionally experience such delightful intimacy with our Bridegroom that all problems seem negligible, but that's not usually the way it is.

Tending to our relationship with Christ, however, does have its rewards. Naturally. When we live close to Him, our lives will be more whole—holy—because we are living according to the purpose for which He created us. Friendship with Jesus provides a sense of strength, significance, and security that allows us to survive and even thrive on this side of heaven.

OUR AMPLE RESOURCES

When we focus on works and our motive to pursue the Lord is out of line, we may be trying to get from Him what He says He's already given. So we should occasionally ask ourselves whether we now possess what we're seeking.

For example, I used to pray, "God, please be with us as we gather here to worship You." Or, "Be with me as I travel." Then one day it dawned on me that in doing so, I was asking for what I already had. The Bible says that Jesus will be with us always (Matt. 28:20), that He will be there when two or three come together in His name (Matt. 18:20), and that He'll never leave us (Heb. 13:5). Thus my requests reflected my unbelief instead of my trust in God's promises. From then on, I stopped asking and started thanking God for His presence. Wherever I am, I am conscious that He is present, even when I don't feel His presence.

Is this quibbling over semantics? I don't think so. My actions are determined by whether I know I have something or am seeking to get it.

And look at how much we have: "His divine power has given us everything we need for life and godliness" (2 Pet. 1:3, NIV). The word is *everything,* not part. The tense of the verb indicates that the action has happened and the effects continue—the giving has taken place and the results are perpetually in effect for us.

We who have received the gift of salvation have at our disposal all the resources we need to be God's vibrant, godly people. We inherit them by being born into the family of God. They are the benefits of our relationship with Him. This makes a world of difference when we think about nurturing intimacy with God. We realize that we don't have to beg for or strive to get what He's already gift-wrapped and presented to us. We simply accept it. Now. And every *now* for the rest of our lives.

But what about Bible study, prayer, worship, and other spiritual activities? Well, of course, those who nurture intimacy with their Abba participate in them, and in the following chapters, we'll note that. The reason for engaging in them, however, is to enjoy to the maximum the relationship He's made possible. We want to cherish the Giver and the gifts He's already given. We seek to nurture intimacy with God primarily because we love Him.

THE GREATEST INCENTIVE

I've seen love's power to motivate. On our wedding day, Lowell didn't draw up a list of demands about how I was to conduct myself as his wife. He didn't issue ultimatums or threats, saying that I had to follow certain rules or he'd stop loving me. If he had done so, perhaps in the fervor of my young love, I'd have tried to jump through the hoops he rolled out. Knowing myself as I do, I suspect that before long I'd have come to resent his conditional love and lack of acceptance. I know I'd eventually have lost motivation and energy to try to please him.

The reality of my life is that my husband deeply loves me—I'm amazed at the strength of his devotion. Because of this, rather than talking of duty, he has overwhelmed me with his love. The result is that I just naturally respond with love for him. I enjoy doing things that please him. Scratch his back. Make his favorite foods. Listen to him. Care for him.

Likewise, love is the basis of my fellowship with God. Since I began to understand His great love for me, my relationship with Christ has never been the same. I've fallen so madly in love with Jesus that it colors every aspect of my life. Of course, I'm not scared to death of

Him. Though I'm not perfect, I no longer carry guilt around because I know His forgiveness. Knowing I am truly forgiven, I've become a better forgiver. I'm free to be honest with myself about who I am and what I need from Him. I still want, with all my heart, to please my Friend, but love makes His yoke easy and His burden light. I no longer think of Him in terms of duty.

I'm not bitter about the legalism of my early years because I have found this statement true: "Love born of duty is not yet real love. It can, however, lead to it. . . . If we lack love, we cannot pretend to have it, nor force ourselves into it. All we can do is ask it of God, believing that he will give it to us."[10]

To be God's intimate, a close follower of Jesus Christ, is to live under the discipline of the Holy Spirit who teaches, guides, convicts, motivates, and much more. It is to enroll in His school voluntarily as one who loves the Teacher, not as a reluctant student in a system of compulsory education.

PART II

UNDERSTANDING GOD

For I desire and delight in . . . the knowledge of and acquaintance with God more than burnt offerings (Hos. 6:6, Amplified Bible).

CHAPTER 5

PREVENT IDOLATRY

erhaps you've said to somebody, "You say you love me, but you don't even know me." When you make that statement, you're expressing your conviction that authentic love requires a certain degree of understanding. Truly, the depth of our relationship with another, including God, is directly tied to how well we know each other.

The love in my marriage is real only to the extent that my husband and I honestly understand one another. I can look back over my life with Lowell and see that, at first, I loved what I thought or hoped he was or would become. (Happily, my conviction that he'd be a good husband proved true.) But today I know what he thinks, feels, believes, and does significantly more than I did during our courtship. As a result, I believe my love for him is more genuine because I accept his true self and not just a figment of my imagination. I think he would say the same about me.

You and I can't have intimacy with another without honest knowledge. Our definition makes this obvious: two people's close, loving, satisfying relationship that results from mutual self-disclosure, deep understanding, and appreciative acceptance of their essential and authentic selves. Thus, the greater our willingness to know and be known, the greater is our potential for intimacy.

Likewise, our relationship with God will be only as authentic as is our concept of Him. You and I must love God as He is, or our intimacy with Him is a delusion, no matter how gloriously emotional our spiritual experiences may be.

WE REFLECT THE GOD WE WORSHIP

Many folks in America may pay lip service to an entity they label "God" because being a tad religious is culturally acceptable or even commended. But who they call God may not be much like the God of Scripture. And that's a grave situation. A. W. Tozer wrote,

> What comes into our minds when we think about God is the most important thing about

us. . . . We tend by a secret law of the soul to move toward our mental image of God. . . . That our idea of God correspond as nearly as possible to the true being of God is of immense importance. . . . The idolatrous heart . . . substitutes for the true God one made after its own likeness. . . . The essence of idolatry is the entertainment of thoughts about God that are unworthy of Him. . . . The idolater simply imagines things about God and acts as if they were true."[1]

That is one of the most powerfully motivating statements I have ever read. Tozer's analysis of the importance of thinking right about God rings true for me. I have come to believe that a large part of maturing in faith is informing and adjusting my view of God so that it increasingly conforms to who He really is. Since I began to think about the "secret law of the soul," I've noticed that what I see in myself or other Christians inevitably reflects our understanding of who God is. I'm not talking about what we Christians *say* the Lord is like; it's easy enough for us to mouth creeds and spout Bible verses. The genuine indicator of our doctrine is our response to Him and to life.

When Lowell's and my son, Toben, was a baby, he didn't sleep much. The books told me that infants snooze most of the day and night, but not our little guy. At almost a year old, he still didn't sleep through the night. During that time, I was beginning to feel as if I'd never feel rested again. It may sound silly, but this became a spiritual issue for me. (The weary will understand how large little things can become.)

I prayed about the problem: "Lord, let this child sleep longer at night. Let me sleep longer at a stretch." Nothing changed—at least not very quickly.

I wondered whether I lacked faith or had unconfessed sin in my life. Mostly, I questioned the ways of God: How could God love me and not allow me a couple of nights of uninterrupted rest? Yet as I rocked my precious infant, I sang to him, "Jesus loves me, this I know; for the Bible tells me so." Obviously, my professed belief about God and my practical behavior were poles apart, but back then it never dawned on me that what came out of my mouth—words about God's love—was inconsistent with what was in my heart—wondering if He really did care about my exhaustion.

My friend—I'll call her Karen—had the same kind of experience. She was a gifted woman who spoke at small evangelistic gatherings whenever she had the opportunity. She explained to others how they could experience God's forgiveness and be assured of eternal life. But she confessed to me that she didn't think God would ever allow her to minister to large groups. Why not? I asked her. Because she had committed what she considered an almost unforgivable sin in her early adult life. She could effectively tell about the concept of God's forgiveness, but she wasn't living in the personal reality of Him as her forgiver. Somehow she couldn't believe her God was able to pardon *her*. She proved David Seamands' statement that "A wrong concept of God leads to a faulty concept of what God wants from us."

Do you see how our practical view of God is reflected in our worries, joys, fears, love, guilt, patience, anger, and other emotions and attitudes? And how that practical view is often inconsistent with our theoretical view? What we do, the way we communicate, our estimate of ourselves, and how we relate to people ultimately find their root in what we really believe about our Creator. I see it as a good exercise to ask myself from time to time, What does the way I think, feel, act, and react say about my view of God?

I also find myself pondering others' concepts of the Lord. One night I watched a television news show. A reporter was interviewing a preacher. He cut to clips of the man jabbing his finger toward a teenage audience while he screamed a message of hellfire and damnation. Asked later about his alleged cruelty toward the young residents at the group home he operated, the minister referred to the proverb that to spare the rod is to spoil the child. He noted that evil is bound up in the heart of some kids and must be beaten out of them. If that required leaving bruises on their adolescent bodies, so be it. A righteous, law-giving God was on his side.

I wanted to see tears in the preacher's eyes. I wanted to find a trace of compassion in his words, the kind of compassion I hear in Jesus' heartbroken lament over Jerusalem (Matt. 23:37). I wondered where and how gentleness, patience, grace, and love fit into his view of God.

I think also of an acquaintance of mine who doesn't seem to know how to deal with the difficult circumstances of her life. She denies a lot of her own hurt and weakness. She's harshly critical of herself and has a difficult time forgiving herself for not being perfect. She is highly unrealistic in her demands on her husband and children, often venting her bad temper on them. She believes in God, but she has many questions about the nature of His love. She views Him primarily as legalistic, rigid, and demanding. She, of course, never measures up to the expectations she thinks He has for her. She thinks of Him as being much like her own capricious and abusive father.

WHAT IS YOUR GOD LIKE?

How can you tell what your view of God is? Look at your response to others and to yourself for a clue. The way you treat your children often finds its origin in the way you think God deals with you. Your relationship with your spouse may mirror how you think the heavenly Bridegroom treats you. Or the following exercise may help give you just a glimpse of how you think about God.

Let's say a professing Christian from your church has been fired from a job because he tampered with the books and pocketed his employer's money. The evidence is irrefutable. How would you respond to him?

You could react in at least one of three ways: One is to say, "Let's remove his name from the membership roll of the church. He violated one of the Ten Commandments, and he ought to be punished. He's definitely not welcome in our home anymore." Or you might react, "The Bible says not to judge but to believe the best about everybody. The man probably feels so bad about this mistake that I think we should just forgive him and act as if the whole thing never happened." A third response is gently to confront the man with his sin and deal with his need to confess it to God (Gal. 6:1). You may even counsel him to make restitution. All the while, you do whatever you can to help him put his life in order, and you show him love and support in practical ways. You let him know you will walk with him for as long as he needs your encouragement.

These three reactions stem from three different views of God. The first reaction indicates a belief that righteousness and truth are the fore-most Christian values. The primary focus is on God's holiness. The second response demonstrates a view that love is the predominant divine attribute and that the Lord is merciful, kind, tenderhearted, and forgiving. In the third scenario, God is understood as being both gracious and true, righteous and merciful, loving and just.

Saying that God *primarily* expresses one of His attributes more than another is untrue. He doesn't temporarily put one aspect of His character on hold so that He can act out another. He is all that He is at all times. Unlike us, He can act in such a way that seemingly contradictory qualities are perfectly compatible in Him. If our knowledge of God approaches some degree of accuracy, we will be more likely to reflect both grace and justice by acting and speaking truth in love (Eph. 4:15).

HAVE THOUGHTS WORTHY OF GOD

Because the world is too much with us, most of us have a hard time keeping clear on who God is. We think we have God figured out and our beliefs are pretty strong, and then real life hits us. Our circumstances tilt on us, and we have a hard time keeping our view of God right side up. Before Toben's birth, I thought I strongly believed in God as my loving Father—after all, He'd blessed us with a child in the seventh year of our marriage. After Toben's birth, however, I wasn't so sure of His compassion. The reality of fatigue pointed out the difference between what I knew in theory as opposed to what I knew with practical, unshakable conviction.

What we believe about God is what we believe about Him when life isn't rosy. Clearly His character doesn't change just because we find ourselves in the midst of problems or confusion. Even though the Bible explains that His attributes are immutable, too often when our situation is unstable, we tend to act as if God has changed. So we respond as if He isn't big enough or powerful enough or wise enough or loving enough to meet us at our point of need. "The essence of idolatry is the entertainment of thoughts about God that are unworthy of Him," as Tozer pointed out.

My thoughts about God became a bit more worthy of Him somewhere between the time my son gave me fits because of his minimum need for sleep and the day my husband and I had to admit our twelve-year-old daughter to a psychiatric hospital. In the intervening years, I had meditated long and hard on Isaiah 9:6 and had begun to grasp the fact that the kind of God I serve is a wise, wonderful Counselor, a mighty, powerful God and a loving, eternal Father. To me. All the time. In every circumstance. Whether it was obvious or hidden. So, on those soul-piercing days that surrounded the diagnosis of our daughter's serious disorders, I clung white-knuckled to my Prince of Peace. And I chose to believe that He is a wonderful, caring God who doesn't leave me or forsake me even when my heart is breaking.

That doesn't mean I didn't feel the anguish intensely. Many times, with tears running down my face, I said, "Lord, You are my wise Counselor even though I can't comprehend why you permitted this to happen. I believe You are almighty God in spite of the fact that I haven't seen You exercise Your power to heal. I trust You as my tender, compassionate Father though I don't feel Your love in this. I claim Your peace and comfort in this painful situation."

Who He is was enough for me back then, and still is today. What I knew of Him sustained me, and I came to know Him more intimately in that school of suffering than I had ever known Him before. I learned in my heart what I'd had in my head; I proved in experience what I'd expressed as my belief. And I loved Him more than ever because He did and does not fail me. I recognized Him as my intimate Friend.

If we don't enjoy intimacy with God, perhaps it's because, as somebody said, God created us in His image and then we returned the favor and created Him in ours. Perhaps we've embraced an unattractive caricature rather than the reality of our lovely Lord. Maybe we've seen Him as a humorless despot, a hard-to-please master, an exacting judge, a cold husband. And it's hard to love somebody like that.

The kind of God who captures our hearts, however, is the forgiving Jesus, the compassionate Christ, the faithful Advocate, the convicting Comforter, the sufficient Savior, the protective Shepherd, the enabling Lord, the exemplary Teacher, the just King. Surely we can't help adoring such an attractive Person. Yes, if we want to nurture intimacy with God, we'll want increasingly to know Him as He is.

CHAPTER 6

EMBRACE THE WORD

I find it poignant that Jesus hung nude on a cross. That nakedness, though more than a symbol, nevertheless symbolizes for me the honesty and vulnerability with which God exposes His heart and essence. It shows the lengths to which He goes to reveal Himself to us. That's good news as we seek to nurture intimacy with God.

J. I. Packer says that the extent to which we know a person "is more directly the result of their allowing us to know them than of our attempting to get to know them. . . . It is they, not we, who decide whether we are going to know them or not."[1] We never need to worry that God won't allow us to know Him. He is never at fault for any lack of intimacy we have with Him.

If our intimacy with God requires honest knowledge and understanding, how do we get to know God as He is? We accept His revelation of Himself in Christ, in Scripture, and through the Holy Spirit. We simply receive those three gifts of His self-disclosure. In this chapter, we shall look at the first two.

JESUS—GOD WITH SKIN

If we want to know what God is like, a good place to start is to look at Jesus Christ. Jesus reveals God's love and commitment to us. He is the Father's means of bringing His rebellious children back into the family. He is the Groom who came to woo and win His bride.

John tells us that the Word, the God who spoke the universe into being at the beginning of time, became flesh by taking on a human body (John 1:14). Jesus explained the reason for His incarnation:

> "For God so loved the world that He gave His only begotten Son, that whoever believes in Him should not perish but have everlasting life. For God did not send His Son into the world to condemn the world, but that the world through Him might be saved. He who

believes in Him is not condemned; but he who does not believe is condemned already, because he has not believed in the name of the only begotten Son of God" (John 3:16–18).

The Gospels show that He lived on our globe in that spot we call the Middle East. He ate and drank and slept. He worked, attended parties, laughed, and cried. He got tired and experienced the kind of temptations we do. He hugged children, rebuked hypocritical religious leaders, and explained to the Samaritan woman that He was the Messiah. Feeling compassion for the needs of people, He performed miracles—He made wine to prevent embarrassment at a wedding, fed the hungry, healed the sick, and raised the dead. He taught and prayed and bested the experts in every theological discussion. Because He didn't fit the mold or conform to preconceived ideas of what God's Christ would be like, He was rejected. He was scorned, falsely accused, condemned by a prejudiced jury, tortured with a crown of thorns and beatings, and crucified. He died saying, "Forgive them for they don't know what they're doing." He was buried, yet resurrected three days later. He returned to heaven where He lives to intercede for us, and someday He'll let us join Him there.

The relationship that is ours to nurture begins when we receive Jesus Christ as our own personal Savior. You and I are not arrogant to claim we know God. We don't overstep our bounds when we believe that what He says is true and that He's delivered what He's pledged to give us.

But where is it that we learn what God is like, how Jesus lived on earth, and what He's promised? How do we gain the knowledge of the Lord that allows our relationship with Him to deepen? The Bible. The written Word is God's self-revelation, and it tells us more about Him than we have the ability to comprehend. He instructs us through our personal study of Scripture. To get closer to Jesus, we need to allow Him to teach us what He's said and then to receive what we learn wholeheartedly.

SCRIPTURE—GOD'S LETTER

Israel's King David, called a man after God's own heart, loved the Lord and His Word. He wrote about the importance of Scripture:

> The law of the Lord is perfect, converting
>   the soul;
> The testimony of the Lord is sure,
>   making wise the simple;
> The statutes of the Lord are right, rejoicing
>   the heart;
> The commandment of the Lord is pure,
>   enlightening the eyes. . . .
> More to be desired are they than gold,

Yea, than much fine gold;
Sweeter also than honey and the honeycomb.
Moreover by them Your servant warned,
And in keeping them there is great reward
    (Ps. 19:7–11).

From David's description of Scripture, we get the idea that he couldn't get enough of it. He said that a godly person will meditate on it in the day and during sleepless nights (Ps. 1:2).

The most significant character of both the Old and New Testaments also confirmed the priority of God's Word. Jesus said people are blessed when they know it and do what it says (Luke 11:28). He stated that truth makes people free (John 8:32). His follower, Paul, wrote that we have hope "through endurance and the encouragement of the Scripture" (Rom. 15:4, NIV). Peter said that we believers have been granted everything we need for life and godliness through our knowledge of Jesus Christ. "He has given to us his very great and precious promises, so that through them you may participate in the divine nature and escape the corruption in the world caused by evil desires" (2 Pet. 1:3–4, NIV). According to Peter, if we are not growing in intimacy and likeness to Christ (and we do become like our intimate friends), we may conclude that either we don't know God's Word or we're not accepting its revelation. The witness of these men is that you and I must become deeply acquainted with Him through the Bible if we want to be intimate with God.

A Love Letter

This does not happen, however, with sporadic or brief involvement in study. If we approach Scripture hit-and-run, we may end up thinking that God strikes down every lying Christian as He did Ananias and Sapphira. Or we may suppose He heals every person because He restored the blind man's sight. In reality, the Bible shows that the God who punishes sin is also longsuffering toward His sinful people. It tells us that the Great Physician didn't heal Paul though he'd asked for it. Only consistent time in the Word gives us a balanced perspective and refines our view of God so that we can worship Him more nearly as He is, rather than a false concept we label "God."

So we read Scripture asking, "What does this tell me about the One whose love I prize more than any other's? What does it say about His character? What clues does it give about what I can do to give Him sheer pleasure?"

I think we're to read the Bible something like I read Lowell's letters to me during our courtship. The two of us met in college. Since we didn't live near each other, summers meant a separation. So we wrote daily to each other all through June, July, and August. Our relationship grew with the help of the United States postal system. Every day I waited anxiously for the mail carrier (who happened to be my dad) to arrive. When Lowell's letter was in my hand, I eagerly devoured its content. Then I read it again. And again. I pondered every nuance. Periodically, I reread his old letters—especially on Sundays when there wasn't a mail delivery. Since I was so in love, it never crossed my mind to not read those love letters or to let them lie unopened for days at a time.

That makes me wonder how God feels when our Bibles go unopened or are read out of duty or in bits and pieces. Does He feel as if we've stamped "Return to Sender" on His love letter to us? To ignore His Word is to miss out on what the Lord wants to tell us about Himself and close off the possibility of getting to know Him as He is and to love Him more.

Though we can hear this idea and even accept it as true, sometimes it's hard to be faithful in Bible reading. How do we overcome that? Do we grab ourselves by the scruff of the neck and force ourselves to wade through a chapter a day? How do we keep this from being a dull routine we do out of a sense of duty? Is there a way to develop the habit of regular, significant time in the Bible apart from exercising strong self-effort?

That's not how it worked for me. Let me explain how I've come to spend consistent time in reading and meditating on God's Word.

A God-given Habit

First, I was convinced of my need to know God through Scripture; I had no doubt about it. So I began to pray each day, "Lord, today I need to know what You've said to me in Your Word. You said that You will give me the desire and ability to do what You want me to do. I'm counting on You to create in me a yearning to read my Bible today. Help me recognize the opportunities You'll give me today to spend some time in study." In the course of the day, I'd remind Him that I was awaiting His drawing me away to meet Him. As I talked to Him, I was confident that Philippians 2:13 really is true, that obedience to Him results from His motivating and enabling me.

What a joy it was when every day the Lord faithfully granted my request. During the morning, afternoon, or evening, I would feel His gentle nudge in my spirit, and I realized that it was time for my appointment to encounter Him. I responded to Him by grabbing my Bible and reading it. This went on day after day until consistent reading in the Word became a habit. This wasn't and isn't a matter of discipline for me, it's more a matter of trusting the Holy Spirit to direct me and then cooperating with Him by acting on the motivation He's giving. I spend time studying Scripture because I want to, not because I have to.

I admit that there were days when I ig-

nored the now-is-a-good-time-to-meet-Me message that He planted in my thinking. When I
failed to respond to Him, I confessed it as sin.
Then I asked Him to continue His good work
in my life, kept on acknowledging that He was
the provider of motivation to read the Word,
and trusted that He would keep on prompting
me to spend daily time with Him.

I rarely talk to God about helping me take
time for reading the Bible at this point in my
life. Studying Scripture is almost second nature
to me now. If I miss that, I feel as if I'm missing
a day's worth of meals—I sense a soul-hunger
for the Word.

BENEFITING FROM OTHERS' INSIGHTS

In addition to learning more about Christ
from Scripture, I've also found that I can learn
much about Him from Bible teachers and good
Christian literature. My understanding of who
God is has been tremendously boosted by such
books as Hannah Whitall Smith's *The God of
All Comfort,* A. W. Tozer's *The Knowledge of
the Holy,* and J. I. Packer's *Knowing God.* I can
say, when folks ask me what's been the greatest
aid to my spiritual walk, that it's been reading
the Bible and solid books. Up through my twenties, teachers in conferences, camps, and churches
shed light on my spiritual life; but in the last

two decades, my main source of spiritual food has come through print.

I'm glad for modern technology that offers the Bible and Bible studies on audio recordings to those who have trouble reading. But, however the Word comes to us, the Holy Spirit stands ready to make it personally alive. I believe, if we trust Him to, we'll find that He'll give us joy in reading and hearing God's Word.

I think of the story Jesus told about a rich man who died and landed in a place of torment. Feeling wretchedly miserable, he begged God that a poor man named Lazarus, who had died and gone to Abraham's bosom, be sent to his five brothers back on earth to warn them to repent and so avoid the fate he suffered. God refused the man's request, saying that if they wouldn't listen to Moses and the prophets (the available Scriptures in Jesus' day), they wouldn't listen to one resurrected poor man who came talking truth to them (Luke 16:20ff).

The point of this story is not about wealth and poverty or the need for compassion and charity—though these are vital interests to Christians. The clear message is this: If we don't read the inspired biblical writers, we have cut ourselves off from our means of knowing God, from checking our concept of Him against who He really is as revealed in Scripture.

CHAPTER 7

ENGAGE
THE
SPIRIT

You and I can't have intimacy with the Lord apart from the ministry of the Holy Spirit in our lives. He, along with Scripture, relates to us who God is and His magnificent promises. Truth would be incomprehensible to us if the Spirit did not enable us to understand and apply it. "The man without the Spirit does not accept the things that come from the Spirit of God, for they are foolishness to him, and he cannot understand them, because they are spiritually discerned" (1 Cor. 2:16). As Martin Luther stated, "The Spirit is needed for the understanding of Scripture and every part of Scripture."

Realizing how vital the Holy Spirit is to my relationship with God makes me glad I live on this side of Pentecost. There have been times when I've wished I had lived when Jesus walked on the earth. How close I would have felt to Him if only I could have walked around Israel with Him, watched Him work, and asked Him questions.

On second thought, I'm glad I wasn't there because when I read the Gospels, I see that the disciples who walked around with Jesus seemed to be in a fog most of the time. After three years, they didn't have a clue about the Messiah and His mission. When He spoke to them of His upcoming death, they couldn't conceive of it. Peter was brash enough to scold Him for even entertaining the idea (Matt. 16:22). And Jesus' half-brothers didn't believe in Him until after His resurrection (John 7:5). The truth is, the people who knew Jesus best knew Him a whole lot better after He returned to His Father. Only then did they comprehend what He'd been about.

That's not what I would have expected. After all, when people die, our relationship with them doesn't grow. We may remember them and even mentally rehearse the good times we'd had together; but as the years pass, we're saddened to realize that we've forgotten a lot about them that we don't wish to lose: her scent, the sound of his chuckle, the way she looked (pictures don't do her justice). One of the hardest things I've experienced in dealing with the death of a couple of my dear friends is that my memory of their image and essence has faded over time, though I didn't want it to.

I would think that through the years the memories Jesus' followers had would slowly diminish after He returned to His Father. They might have read the Old Testament passages, especially the Messianic parts, and even the biography of His life that four different men penned. But could words on paper advance their growing passion for and personal experience with the living Lord?

WHO IS THE HOLY SPIRIT?

The crucial factor in making Christ alive and real to them, even years after His ascension, was the ministry of the Holy Spirit. The book of Acts records how the One He had sent helped the first-century people of God grow in grace, knowledge of, and intimacy with the ascended Jesus. The Spirit, even today, is the key to knowing God as He is, but He seems to be the most misunderstood person of the Trinity.

Some think of Him as an influence or a force, but He's a person, not a thing. The Holy Spirit is God who reveals and glorifies Jesus in us believers today, just as Jesus revealed and glorified the Father while He was on Earth. He filled the church on the day of Pentecost. He now indwells every believer. And according to Romans 8:9, if you or I don't have the Spirit, we don't belong to Christ.

Before His death, Jesus had promised the Holy Spirit to His disciples as another comforter like Himself (John 14:16). He said the Spirit would guide them into all truth (John 16:13), testify concerning Him (John 15:26), and remind them of all He'd said so that they would be accurate witnesses of Him (John 14:26).

According to Jesus, after He went back to be with His Father, He wouldn't keep in touch with His people by sending messages down to Earth in the way a football coach sends in plays from the sidelines to his quarterback on the field. He, by the Spirit, would be right there on the field with His team, wherever they were. That's why Jesus could say truthfully, "I tell you the truth. It is to your advantage that I go away; for if I do not go away, the Helper will not come to you; but if I depart, I will send Him to you" (John 16:7).

How could He possibly say that His departure was "profitable—good, expedient, advantageous," as *The Amplified Bible* puts it? Because the Holy Spirit whom He sent would not be limited as He was. When our Savior walked around the Middle East, His body imposed certain restrictions on Him. He could only be in one place at a time; when He was in Jerusalem,

He could not be in Capernaum. Only so many people could get near Him at a time. His voice could not be heard beyond a certain distance. Jesus could be *with* people before His ascension, but never *in* them. Because of the indwelling Holy Spirit, however, the resurrected Christ could actually take up His residence in the bodies of believers (John 14:17).

THE MINISTRY OF THE SPIRIT

Early in my Christian life, I was thoroughly confused about the ministry of the Holy Spirit. I had committed myself to Jesus when I was about five, and I believed He lived in my heart—a simple act of faith for me. But accepting the Holy Spirit's presence and power into my life? That seemed to me to be an altogether different matter.

I thought I had to plead with Him to come into me. I felt I had to make a unique surrender to the Spirit that was totally different from my yielding to Jesus. Before I could expect the Holy Spirit to control me, I thought I needed a faith distinct from that which made my salvation real to me.

Through studying the Bible, I have come to believe, as A. W. Tozer wrote, that "all of God does all that God does." When the Son came into my life, so did the Father and the Holy Spirit. In accepting the Son, I've received the

Spirit also. I accept what Thomas Arnold said, "He who does not know God the Holy Spirit cannot know God at all." First Corinthians 2:10–11 explains the importance of the indwelling Spirit in developing our relationship with God: "The Spirit searches all things even the deep things of God. For who among men knows the thoughts of a man except the man's spirit within him? In the same way no one knows the thoughts of God except the Spirit of God" (NIV).

As I meditated on these verses one day, I considered the fact that nobody knows me as my spirit does. No human being knows me better than I know myself, though I've wanted people to understand me better, to feel my feelings, and to think my thoughts. I've wished they could have experienced my life's events and my reactions to them because those things shaped me into the person I am. However, I've resigned myself to the fact that others can never completely understand me because they don't live in my skin.

People can't read my mind, just as I can't read theirs. No matter how much we talk, there are limits to how much we can enter another's thoughts and feelings. We can never crawl into another's heart and brain. The spirit of a soul-bonded friend is a separate entity from my spirit. I may understand partially, but never completely, what is going on inside another person.

A second thought leaped out at me from

the Corinthian passage: You and I can know the Lord better than we can know another human being—even one who lives with us. Because of the Holy Spirit, vertical intimacy—between God and us—can be greater than horizontal intimacy—between us and others. Since the Spirit of God has taken up residence in us, the One who knows God's thoughts lives in us to reveal Him to us.

Paul tells us our Father's purpose in all this: We have received "the Spirit who is from God that we may understand what God has freely given us. . . . We have the mind of Christ" (1 Cor. 2:12, 16).

GETTING THE SPIRIT'S PERSPECTIVE

To have the mind of Christ doesn't mean that we know everything about God or that we know as much as He does. Our finite minds can't begin to comprehend the Infinite. His thoughts are indeed above our thoughts, higher than the heavens are above the Earth (Isa. 55:8–9). To have the mind of Christ means that we have been given some capacity to see life from His perspective. Because of the Spirit, we believers can grasp, in effective and practical ways, those truths that are consistent with the character of God. He enables us to understand and accept as reliable the revelation in Scripture about God's attributes—that He is infinite, present, just, loving, wise, and powerful.

The Spirit, who knows God and reveals Him to us, also knows us intimately. Understanding us perfectly, He knows us better than we could ever know ourselves. For that reason, He can point out those things in us that are incongruent with godliness. When we engage in acts and attitudes of unfairness, meanness, ignorance, and weakness, He sets off a "sin alarm system" in our souls, as a friend of mine calls it. As Jesus said, He convicts of sin and righteousness and judgment (John 16:8). In His role as Teacher, He shows us our ignorance. As our Comforter, He encourages us with God's love and promises. In short, He reveals God to us in an intensely intimate way that, if we permit, transforms our understanding of and relationship with Him.

I realize that many times the Holy Spirit has used the Word to give me a new perception of who God is. When I've experienced pain or suffering, He has taught me from the Bible that God is indeed "the God of all comfort" (2 Cor. 1:3). I remember when a person told me he didn't like me. He made accusations in general terms but didn't seem able to define specifically what I had done to elicit his ill will. He couldn't tell me any ways in which I had been unfair, thoughtless, or unkind to him. He alluded to the fact that who I was, not my deeds, bugged him. He did express his discomfort with my faith in Christ. Though I searched my heart and asked my husband's help to assess the situation, neither he nor I could pinpoint a reason for the man's criticism or negative opinion of me.

I was pulverized. And it wasn't hard for me to think that if one person found me annoying, perhaps God didn't like me too well either.

A few hours later, I took refuge in the Word. I sat down to my daily Bible reading and located the passage for that day, Romans 8. Suddenly my heart soared as I saw verse 31: "If God is for us, who can be against us?" I realized that God's love for me hadn't changed just because somebody didn't like me. So though I'd read that sentence many times before, never had it felt so tangibly, soothingly mine. The Holy Spirit confirmed the truth of the Word to me *personally,* and I was comforted.

Years later, when confronted with my daughter's mental illness, I was again in need of a deeper understanding of God's sufficiency to meet my needs. After testing my child extensively, the psychologist said, "I hate to tell you this, but when people are like this at thirteen, they are like this at twenty-three and thirty-three." She had just diagnosed my daughter's mental illness as incurable, but perhaps treatable. Hearing that, I felt an emotional pain that actually made me hurt in the spot right below my diaphragm.

In the days that followed, I read Habakkuk. I saw how the prophet wrestled with what seemed to be a lack of answer to his prayers. I understood his dilemma; I knew what it was to pray for a long time without seeing the results I'd hoped for. Habakkuk, however, came to understand that God was in control of the affairs of nations and people; He was actively involved even when it appeared that He wasn't aware of His people's plight.

I realized my Abba knew *exactly* what was happening to me and my child. I read His words, "The just shall live by faith" (2:4). I saw I was to live by faith. Not by sight. Not by feelings. Not by prayers being answered the way that suited me. The Holy Spirit seemed to nudge me to trust in the magnificent character of my sovereign God and His allowances in my life, even though I didn't understand His reasons. I began to understand that, because He is merciful and righteous and knows the end from the beginning, He is totally dependable. In this way, the indwelling Holy Spirit took that Scripture and made God real and relevant to me in my heartbreaking situation.

THE SPIRIT AND THE WORD

The Holy Spirit uses the Word of God as His tool to enlighten us about who God is and change us into the image of Christ. I find it interesting to note that the role of the Spirit, as Jesus defined it, and the ministry of the Word, as noted in 2 Timothy 3:16, are the same: "All

Scripture is given by inspiration of God, and is profitable for doctrine, for reproof, for correction, for instruction in righteousness that the man of God may be complete, thoroughly equipped for every good work." That description of what the Word does—teaching, rebuking, correcting, training—and Jesus' statements in John's Gospel of what the Spirit does are remarkably parallel, aren't they?

Paul also linked the Spirit and the Word. He spoke of "words taught by the Spirit, expressing spiritual truths in spiritual words" (1 Cor. 2:13, NIV). Those Spirit-taught and expressed truths are recorded in the Bible. Furthermore, the apostle called the Word of God the sword of the Spirit, His offensive weapon for securing victory for believers (Eph. 6:17).

Thus, the Word and the Spirit are inseparably bound together in this matter of knowing God—in fact, in every aspect of our spiritual birth and life. We become aware of the commands of God through the Scripture, and the Spirit convinces us of their validity and shows us that we have broken them.

The Holy Spirit initiates and brings about our entry into the family of God, He fits us by means of the Word for that relationship. We study the Bible's long lists of good and evil behaviors, gaining understanding about the holiness of God, and the Holy Spirit reveals which of them we need to confront if we are to be like Him.

We read that God loves us and then realize that "the love of God has been poured out in our hearts by the Holy Spirit, who was given us" (Rom. 5:5). Furthermore, "the manifestation of the Spirit is given to each one for the profit of all," and we as a group "are being built together for a habitation of God in the Spirit" (1 Cor. 12:7 and Eph. 2:22). What we learn in Scripture concerning our place among God's chosen people, we experience as the Holy Spirit gives us not only love for our brothers and sisters in faith but also gifts to build each other up.

Yes, the Holy Spirit enables us believers to discover our Father, Bridegroom, and Friend by helping us understand and discern the Word. We program our minds with the truth (and this is the value of memorizing Scripture), and we can expect the Holy Spirit to remind us of the nature of God at the time we need to comprehend who He wants to be to us. And His voice is not coming from far away, but from within. He's saying, in essence, "Here's who I am. Here's what I will be to you. This is what you can be because of My living in you."

When you think about it, because you and God the Holy Spirit live in the same body, the potential for your being intimate with Him could not be greater.

PART III

UNDERSTANDING MYSELF

Examine and test and evaluate your own selves,
to see whether you are holding to your faith
and showing the proper fruits of it (2 Cor. 13:5,
Amplified Bible).

CHAPTER 8

LOOK BEYOND SKIN DEEP

Our wisdom . . . consists almost entirely of two parts: the knowledge of God and of ourselves," John Calvin wrote at the beginning of *Institutes*. For us to nurture intimacy with God requires that we know not only God as He is but also ourselves as we are.

Yet, when I first read a statement by Bernard of Clairvaux that self-knowledge is the highest knowledge, I immediately resisted the idea. My mind argued that surely the highest knowledge is knowledge of God. The more I pondered the matter, however, the more I began to see that what you and I know about the Lord will have little impact on us unless we understand ourselves.

TRUTH OR CONSEQUENCES

If we don't know who we are, we can't possibly appreciate what God wants and needs to be to us. The more we know ourselves, the greater the possibility we will realize our need for God. Jesus said that the Great Physician cannot apply His healing to those who claim they are well. Only the sick person who feels a need for the doctor calls him, not the one who stubbornly refuses to admit he's ill (Luke 5:31).

Clifford Williams wrote, "The first requirement for accepting God's mercy is that we see ourselves as needing mercy. . . . We must see ourselves as we really are."[1] Unless we get in touch with how self-centered, unforgiving, impatient, complaining, cowardly, or whatever we are, we will likely never know the love relationship that grows by discovering that our heavenly Father accepts us and meets us at our point of need.

Knowing ourselves provides a lot of impetus for seeking God's solution to the stuff we really don't like about ourselves. Unless we are willing to face who we are, we will spend the rest of our lives playing pretend games with ourselves, God, and others. We'll be dishonest, hypocritical, and emotionally and spiritually tied in knots. We'll not experience authentic relationships either with God or with others because we aren't being genuinely ourselves with them. To get intimate with our Friend Jesus, we must take the risk of being real with ourselves about ourselves.

I think of Jim*, an elder in his church. His daughter Marian* is scared of him because of the way he beat her a few years ago when she performed a stupid, dangerous, but not untypical, teenage act. Jim has also called her shameful, derogatory names. Most of all, the young woman feels the pain of her father's conditional acceptance of her. Mature, bright, and sensitive to God, Marian has tried to communicate openly with Jim about the pain and stress she experiences because of his treatment of her. But he doesn't own responsibility for the rift in the father-daughter relationship—it's all her fault. He not only refuses to admit he may be wrong, but he tells her his unloving behavior stems from his obedience to God. How can Jim's relationship with Marian improve without his willingness to take a hard look at how he's contributed to fracturing it? Unless he faces the fact that he's an angry, domineering man, how can he appropriate God's help to overcome his shortcomings?

The truth is that all of us tend to have little tolerance for the raw, cold truth about who we are as sinful creatures in a fallen world. When we think about getting in touch with ourselves,

---

*Names and identities of individuals in this chapter have been changed to protect their privacy.

we may feel threatened. Being imperfect makes most of us squirm with embarrassment. We hate the awareness of our weaknesses. To shine light into the dark corners of our lives can be painful indeed.

"We do not want to look into ourselves because we do not like what we see . . . we are both deceiver and deceived."[2] We may try to hide ourselves from ourselves, preferring to maintain illusions about our own deity. That makes it imperative that we ignore the limits of our finite goodness, wisdom, power, love, and righteousness.

Some folks even use religious activity to keep from facing who they are. When the truth gets close to home, I've seen people in small group Bible studies wriggle out of the discomfort zone they find themselves in. They do this by glibly quoting Scripture in answer to a personal question, or they change the subject by asking for theological clarification about a peripheral issue. Their message comes through loud and clear, "Let's discuss the Bible, but let's not get personal or relevant." But unless we get intensely personal about our authentic selves, we may know much about God but not know Him practically and intimately.

OUR FOUR SELVES

When we seek to know ourselves, we discover that each of us has four areas of self-knowledge.[3] They are 1) the open self, 2) the concealed self, 3) the blind self, and 4) the unknown self.

The *open self* is that part of us that is known by us and others too. This self is recognizable to all and may include information like our height, shape, sex, and the color of our hair and eyes. Other things such as our age, temperament, likes, and dislikes are also often obvious to acquaintances and friends. (The distinguishing difference between friends and acquaintances is more the depth of knowing and appreciating each other than it is the length of time in knowing.)

The *concealed self* is that aspect of ourselves which we know but choose not to reveal to others. We may decide to keep details of our background and upbringing secret. We may work hard to hide our fears, hopes, or fantasies from others. Because gaining others' acceptance drives much of our behavior, we often hide the parts of ourselves we suspect may be unaccepted, belittled, unappreciated, ridiculed, or otherwise negatively received. Thus, we may take great pains to keep these things under wraps.

The *blind self* is known to others but not to us. Often we are unaware of aspects of our personalities which are apparent to others. Counselors can make a decent living just telling clients what they see that the clients don't. All of us are subjective about ourselves to one degree or another; we can't be totally neutral about things concerning ourselves. We lack the objectivity, therefore, to see and assess ourselves accurately.

The poet, Robert Burns, wrote, "O wad some Power the giftie gie us/To see oursels as ithers see us!" But then maybe we don't want to see ourselves as others see us; maybe we desire to stay blind. (Do we want to know what we look like when we're throwing a temper tantrum?) Jesus called this attitude choosing to walk in darkness.

The *unknown self* is the part of us that neither we nor others are aware of. As a result, nobody—including us—understands the roots of this impulse or that motivation, this emotion or that action. We're at a loss to explain it. Sometimes we don't even know what we don't know, yet that unknown fact has an impact on who we are and what we do.

God alone knows everything about every part of us, including our unknown self. Psalm 139 says, "O Lord, you have searched me and you know me. You know when I sit and when I rise; you perceive my thoughts from afar. You discern my going out and my lying down; you are familiar with all my ways. Before a word is on my tongue you know it completely, O Lord" (verses 1–4, NIV). Furthermore, the Bible tells us that we are written on the palms of God's hands (Isa. 49:16). Jesus says that He knows even the number of hairs on our heads (Luke 12:7).

The encouraging aspect about this is that,

since He already knows us, we can never shock or repulse God by acknowledging to ourselves or to Him what He already knows about us. As J. I. Packer put it, God's love is so utterly realistic that no discovery we may make about ourselves can disillusion Him about us.[4] To quote Williams, "There is one thing, and only one thing, however, that alleviates the pain of seeing ourselves as we really are, and that is knowing that God accepts us. . . . But if we recognize God's acceptance, we will be able to look at and accept our guilty selves. Accepting mercy causes in us a sense of having worth to God, which produces a permanent and profound serenity that cannot be obtained in any other way."[5] With this sure and comforting foundation, we may find the bravery to venture getting acquainted with our blind and unknown selves.

HOW DO WE KNOW OURSELVES?

How do we get in touch with our blind and unknown selves? There are a number of ways.

Personality Profiles

One fairly mechanical means is by using personality tests and profiles. Both those in the human resources and mental health professions regularly ask people to complete profile forms to gain insight into personality. These include Performax, Personal Dynamics Profiles, Taylor-Johnson Temperament Analysis, Minnesota Multi-Phasic, and many others. These can be extremely helpful to those who have never given much thought to who they are.

Have you ever given thought to questions such as: How do I make decisions—by careful analysis or by intuition? Is my tendency toward being organized or disorganized? Am I comfortable in a casual living space or do I require neatness? How do I expend energy—in spurts or evenly over a long period of time? The answers often reflect more the way you came into the world than how you were brought up.

My husband and I have found personality profiles extremely helpful in understanding not only ourselves but also each other. We've come to realize that some of our differences aren't a matter of right or wrong or even strengths or weaknesses, but more of inborn personality traits. Lowell, for example, is more extroverted than me; therefore, it's no wonder he's the one who pushes more to be involved in social events. For some reason, to have this show up on our personality tests has enabled us to be more objective about our individual characteristics.

If you would like to have a personality analysis, you can ask a psychologist to help you. Perhaps your minister or a counselor from your church may be able to accommodate you. Also, you could check with the personnel manager where you work for information on this.

Koinonia

Another and certainly warmer way to discover ourselves is in relationship with people. Friends show us who we are. As Walter Wangerin wrote, "It always takes another person to show me to myself."[6]

I have been gifted with both a husband and a best friend who love me and have provided for me the sense of safety that allows me to be myself with them. I can tell them anything and know that they will gently reflect both the positive and negative aspects of myself back to me in a way that helps me gain perspective on who I am. They have helped my personal growth immeasurably. David Seamands notes that "the kind of honesty and self-knowledge which will bring about lasting changes in our lives *almost always requires another person. It is when we disclose our true, private selves to someone else that we fully come to know ourselves for real.*"[7]

Through my husband, I learned I had a temper. I can't remember having gotten angry very often before I married. Lowell didn't cause my outbursts, though at times I wanted badly to think he did! The reality was that my husband provided me with the security I needed to get in touch with something inside me that I had never before allowed to surface.

James M. Houston wrote,

"I need a soul friend to give me insights into the ways I am deceived or insensitive, or hardened by sin within me. I cannot do it alone. Self-examination can only take me so far. I need others to help expose and help me understand where sin would deceive and confuse me. . . . Often our soul friends can show us the ecology of evil within us, how a particular childhood wound, or fixation of emotion, or emotional frame of mind, have brought the addictions that now enthrall us, coloring and distorting all we do and are. It may be that only the courage and wisdom of true soul friends can expose the ambitions and compulsions that lie behind our addictions to ministry, to pleasing everybody, or to 'being in the limelight.' "[8]

When we get together with people, even in the community of faith, we inevitably run up against things we can't easily love in each other. We see characteristics in them, both good and bad, to which they are blind, and they see our blind spots. In fellowship, or *koinonia* as the early church called it, we are in a wonderful milieu for self-discovery.

Joe* was a placator and didn't realize it. He drove his friends crazy by fishing for compli-

---

* Names and identities of individuals in this chapter have been changed to protect their privacy.

ments, acting indecisively, and changing his mind often. He seemed to have an internal thermometer to measure how cool or warm others were to an idea, and he dressed his comments accordingly. He never realized he was doing this, but it was glaringly evident to his friends.

When a friend cared enough to tell Joe about his annoying actions, Joe responded by telling something about his concealed self: he had been emotionally abused as a child. He had learned early how to placate in order to protect himself against more suffering. This exchange of information deepened Joe's insight about himself.

Though others' perceptions about us can indeed be enlightening, not everything others may say about us is true. The source of the comment is important. Is the person playing amateur psychologist? How well does he know us? Is he spiritually mature and emotionally healthy himself? Does he love us and is he motivated by a desire for our well-being? The value of another's assessment of us usually depends on who they are and how well they know us. We do well to evaluate what somebody may say about us, but then we have the responsibility to keep what's true and toss out the rest.

One day at lunch, a woman told me that I was more tired than I knew. She was right. At another lunch, another woman told me what motivates me. She was dead wrong. The first was a friend who knows me and loves me well; she understood my heavy schedule and observed the physical toll that my many activities were taking on me. The second was a person I'd never spent any time with until that day; she could only guess that I was influenced by the same inner promptings that drove her.

Personality profiles and the input from a spouse, best friend, and those in our *koinonia* are just two routes to self-understanding. We will look at others in following pages. And if you wrestle with the thought that engaging in such introspection is unbiblical and maybe too self-centered, remember these words of Thomas a Kempis: "A humble knowledge of self is a surer way to God than a deep search after learning."[9] We will never be more intimate with God than we are knowledgeable about ourselves.

CHAPTER 9

GET IT DOWN IN WRITING

*T*wo other means to help us know ourselves and thus nurture our intimacy with God are found in two books: the Bible and a personal journal.

Just as Scripture reveals God to us, so it shows us who we are. For each of us, "True knowledge of self comes not from my searching myself but from God searching me."[1] And He uses Scripture to do so.

THE MIRROR OF SCRIPTURE

A few years ago I felt very angry because a teacher had mistreated my son, and in a Christian high school no less. I believed I was totally justified in my response; I called it righteous indignation against sin. That man's behavior was inexcusable, and he deserved not only my censure but punishment from God Himself.

Then I sat down to read my Bible. I came across the verse, "Therefore, my beloved brethren, let every man be swift to hear, slow to speak, slow to wrath; for the wrath of man does not produce the righteousness of God" (James 1:19–20). Now I had seen that statement many times and thought it was a good one. I'd even written several chapters of a book by expanding on the first part of it.

Nevertheless, that morning I found new meaning in it. First, I had to come to grips with the fact that my wrath would not produce godliness; probably resentment and bitterness would be the result. Then very gently, the Holy Spirit began to bring God's thoughts into my mind: The Lord is not pleased with my peevish temper, unrighteous self-pity, or unforgiving attitude. I must let go of my anger, or it will get in the way of my relationship with my Abba and others.

Yes, you and I need the Word to show us who we are and what we do. Though covered over with flesh and skin, layers of good grooming, and etiquette, our hearts are deceitful and desperately wicked (Jer. 17:9). That means that although our friends may be good and faithful to point out sin in our lives, we will inevitably try to put the best face on it. Or we will excuse it: "If you really grasped what's going on here, you would understand why it is all right for me to react as I do." Our misleading hearts will distort even the positive input of friends. They may speak healing words about our worth in God's sight and our good qualities, but we may discount them. We need the Word and the Spirit, therefore, to convince us of the way God sees us.

If we value truth and righteousness, we come to the light of Scripture; but if they make us feel uncomfortable, we avoid that light (John 3:19–21). You and I will shun or seek truth depending upon our commitment to self-understanding. When we are in love with our sins, we may mishandle truth in any of several different ways.

One way is to distort it: "God says He hates divorce, but He also says He delights in giving us good gifts. I know He wants me to be happy, and I can't be happy with you as my wife. I am out of here." This twists the Bible's message to mean that God prizes our happiness above our holiness.

A second way to mishandle truth is by rationalizations (rational lies, a friend calls this). We may make an appeal to a supposedly superior knowledge to which the biblical writers were not privy: "Surely Paul overstated the case when he said my jealousy isn't as bad as witchcraft

and drunkenness. I know it doesn't hurt anybody." Or, "Yes, the Bible condemns fornication
and adultery, but we modern people know that
confining sexual activity to marriage is impossible, if not an outright aberration."

A third means of avoiding truth is to ignore it. I've heard some folks indicate that they
don't want to take in more light because they
don't want to be held accountable to God for
it. This is the what-I-don't-know-won't-hurt-me
stance, and it makes about as much sense as thinking that to ignore a cancerous tumor won't result
in death. Self-determined ignorance is no refuge
from responsibility.

The one who tries to convince us that
truth is relative, dangerous, or requires bending
is the one Jesus called the father of lies, a liar
from the beginning (John 8:44). Satan attempts
to gain his evil, damning goals to ruin us by
convincing us that truth is harmful, painful, en-
slaving, generally bothersome, and to be avoided
whenever possible.

TRUTH MAKES YOU FREE

If we are Christians, we have committed
ourselves to the Lord Jesus Christ who said, "I
am the Truth" (John 14:6). In giving ourselves
to Him, we dedicate ourselves to the truth not
only about Him but about ourselves.

And that truth liberates us: Jesus said, "If

you abide in My word, you are my disciples indeed. And you shall know the truth, and the truth shall make you free. . . . Therefore if the Son makes you free, you shall be free indeed" (John 8:31, 32, 36). Truth frees as light frees, enabling us to function without the restrictions imposed on those who can't see.

If we determine to nurture intimacy with God, who is light, we must know the Word that "is a lamp to my feet/And a light to my path (Ps. 119:105). Otherwise, we will walk in the darkness of the spiritually blind and not have fellowship with the Father (1 John 1:5–7).

By studying Scripture we find out who we are in God's light. We discover that we are forgiven, not under condemnation, seated with Christ in the heavenly places, clothed in His righteousness, and indwelt by the Spirit. We learn that we are secure and significant in our Father, and He is in control of the events of our lives. He gives us spiritual gifts and an important function in the body of Christ.

Scripture is the source of the great and precious promises that enable us to participate in the divine nature (2 Pet. 1:4). These include God's covenant vows to love, protect, guide, comfort, take us to heaven, and much more. They give us the only sure basis for a healthy self-respect because they reveal how important we are to our Abba.

The Bible also uncovers the negative stuff

about us—our transgressions in thought, word, and deed—but we can even feel positive about that. Why? One reason is that our Bridegroom loves us too much to let us live in ignorance about those things that get in the way of the blessings of intimate relationship with Him. Conviction of sin is a marvelous proof of God's grace, and grace is cause for delight.

When the Holy Spirit used the Word to confront the apostle Paul about a sin, he lamented over his sin and his powerlessness in its grip. And though he was dead in his sin, because he saw the mercy of God active on his behalf, he was able to praise Christ for making him alive again (Rom. 7:7–25).

When I was in high school, I experienced being set free through the truth of the Word. From childhood, fear had restricted my life. In reading Scripture, I began to see that being irrationally scared all the time was inconsistent with the relationship I professed to have with Christ. I'm thankful the Lord didn't leave me to wallow in the shame and guilt of that conviction. As I studied, I saw not only that my crippling fear was sinful but also that trusting God would free me from it.

I began to memorize and meditate on Psalm 91, and it slowly healed me. I started to see myself as a protected person who is not alone in frightening situations. Instead I saw that the powerful God is with me. As I looked intently "into the perfect law of liberty," I increasingly experienced the rewards of living free of fear (James 1:25).

Even when God's laws show us to be violators, we have the confidence that those commandments are promises of what we may become in Christ Jesus. We learn that we are to forgive, bear one another's burdens, be kind to each other, edify God's family, grow in grace. Then we realize that He's telling us the kind of behaviors He will produce in our lives, not overnight but little by little, if we will allow the Holy Spirit to control us. So, the Word not only shows us who we are but what we are becoming. The law is a promise and not a threat, for the One who fulfilled the law indwells us to live His life through us. That's the clear, comforting message of the Word.

WRITING YOUR OWN BOOK

In addition to the Bible, another book that helps us understand who we are is the one we write about what we think and feel about life, family, friends, God, profession, fun, and—most of all—about ourselves. This book is often called a personal journal.

A journal is a book in which you keep a personal record of events in your life, of your different relationships, of your response to things, of your feelings about things—of your search to find out who you are and what the meaning of life might be. It is a book in which you carry out the greatest of life's adventures—the discovery of yourself.[2]

I have found writing a journal one of the best ways to gain the self-understanding necessary to nurture my intimacy with God. Another journal-keeper, Morton Kelsey, states this even more strongly: "I doubt whether those who can read and write are able to come to the deep relationship with the divine lover which is possible for them if they do not keep a journal."[3]

If we tend to be perfectionists, we may wonder about the "right" way to keep a journal; but there is no right or wrong way, just our way, to keep it. We may write two sentences or two pages. We may write daily or once or twice a week. What we do is for us to decide. If we want to record the daily temperature, that's our prerogative. We don't even have to worry about neatness since it is for our eyes only.

For a journal to add to our self-understanding, however, we will want to jot down more than the events of our day—the meetings we attended, the people we saw, the food we ate. That's primarily what a diary is all about. A journal may—if we choose—include all that a diary does, but it is more than that. It notes our insights, questions, concerns, and reactions to events. It may contain significant quotes we collect from sermons, books, and magazines. It may record our prayers and prayer list.

For a journal to have any value, we must write truthfully, putting things down as they are, not as we wish they were. If we are honest, keeping a journal can contribute to knowing ourselves in the following ways.

Capturing Ourselves

First, our thoughts, rushing and tumbling through our minds, tend to get away from us Probably all of us have had a thought and said to ourselves, "I've *got* to remember this; this is *good.*" Later, we can't recall that poignant insight or brilliant statement for the life of us. So we do well to fix on paper the ideas and experiences that slip away from us. When we write down what we are thinking, feeling, doing, and believing, we know we have captured a bit of ourselves.

Viewing Ourselves Objectively

Second, seeing things in black and white lets us view what's happening objectively. Madeleine L'Engle wrote, "If I can write things out, I can see them; and they are not trapped within my own subjectivity." Sometimes I've written something down and said to myself, "I didn't know I thought that." Or, "So that's how I really feel!"

I sense that when I think, but am not writing down what I think, I often mentally edit myself. I clean up my perceptions. I don't acknowledge where my mind is going if it begins to wander into uncomfortable or sinful territory. I tend to talk myself into believing that what I'd like to think true of myself or others or even God is indeed what I think of them.

When I take pen and notebook in hand, however, it becomes harder for me to duck and dodge. The ideas come out in a tangible form, and I'm faced with truth at that point. Sometimes I'm pleasantly surprised; other times I'm sadly informed. The important thing is that I get in touch with who I am as a person who wants to relate to God with openness. Richard Foster wrote, "Writing out our concerns helps to clarify things and keep us honest."[4]

I saw this happen with a friend. He had spent decades preserving a mental memorial to his angel-mother. One day, in dealing with personal problems that puzzled and bound him, he began to delve into his relationships by writing in his journal about the significant people in his life. As he wrote about his mom, he praised her to the skies until, unexpectedly, he began to get in touch with darker feelings, feelings of pain and anger because she had not protected him from his abusive father. Realizing this, he was able to deal with his repressed resentment and, as a result, came to experience a great sense of

release through understanding himself and forgiving his mother.

The objectivity involved in writing something down is often a good way to define and
sometimes solve problems. I can be upset and
confused and my thoughts a tangled net tying
up my logic. So I take pen and notebook in hand
and begin to write it all out where I can look
at it squarely. Then I can deal with it calmly
and candidly before my Abba.

Discovering Ourselves

Third, a journal acts as an emotional safety
valve. We can gunny-sack feelings and thoughts
and ignore them for a while—perhaps because
we may think, "I shouldn't feel or think this
way." Sooner or later, however, what we have
worked hard to deny will emerge—perhaps as
fat, depression, verbal or physical abuse, alcohol-
ism, drug dependency, ulcers, migraines, cancer,
or a number of other things.

Writing can help us appropriately express
our hate, anger, fear, or love. Perhaps the most
common example of this is the release that comes
from writing, and then destroying, a scorching
letter to one who has deeply hurt us. Morton
Kelsey wrote, "The journal . . . gives us a safe
way of dealing with our feelings that are often
ready to burst out of us." Telling about people
who lied and acted out of fear and prejudice,

the book of *Acts* does not flatter the first-century church, so it's all right if our book reveals that we are not always shining examples of godliness either.

Sometimes recognizing our emotions motivates us to action. Are we angry? Well, maybe that anger indicates a bitterness we need to confess. Do we hurt for another? Perhaps that compassion must be expressed in deeds.

A RECORD OF OUR JOURNEY

We're in the company of biblical writers when we write a journal. David's psalms record what he thought, felt, and experienced concerning God, himself, others, and his circumstances. He asked the Lord hard questions, vented his hatred of his enemies, questioned God's ways, grieved over his sins, rejoiced in his successes, recorded his insights about creation and human nature, and offered prayers and praise. (And he did it all in poetic form to boot!) His writings are so honest, so in tune with the human condition, that we can identify with him and use his words to express our own deep thoughts and emotions.

Paul's letters to the churches were a kind of journal in which he recorded doctrine, application, information about himself and his colleagues. His prayers and doxologies are spoken today whenever Christians gather.

My journals are certainly emaciated relatives of those of David and Paul, and they aren't inspired. However, they're a vital part of my devotional life. I keep a Bible and a notebook of about the same size together. As I read Scripture, I write anything that grabs my attention: a list of godly (or, perhaps, ungodly) characteristics that I need to be aware of, my reflections on an event, a promise I want to make, a confession of sin, a prayer. Sometimes, if my head is buzzing with a situation that upsets me, I may write in my journal before I read Scripture as a way of clearing my thoughts.

My journals contain a record of my spiritual pilgrimage. They remind me of answered prayer. They contain devotional commentary with a personal application on most of the Bible. (I've been at this a long time now.) They show me who I am before God.

Occasionally, I reread what I've written in years past. Sometimes I want to remind myself to incorporate into the present what God has shown me to be true in the past. I may want to recollect insights I gained years ago on a Scripture passage I'm studying today. I may search them for message ideas. I look for evidence of growth and answered prayer; the encouragement of past victories comfort me when today seems bleak. I get in touch with the real me and what that says about my relationship with God. Whatever I do with today's or yesterday's journals, my experience agrees with that of Morton Kelsey who wrote, "The insights that I recorded stuck with me and were more likely to be integrated into my life than those ideas and experiences that were not written down."[5]

Above all, a personal journal is our personal book of *Acts,* the acts of the Holy Spirit in us. As David McKenna, president of Asbury Theological Seminary, noted, "Wesley and other early Methodists kept journals of their life history. They . . . remembered their spiritual past by tracing the evidence of prevenient grace at work in their lives." He continued, "Reviewing the chapters of our lives . . . we ask the question, 'How was the Spirit of God leading me during this time in my life?' By tracing the movement of the Spirit, even through trauma, tragedy, frustration and failure, we will sing of grace."[6]

We never need fear what we learn about ourselves from either Scripture or our journals. The One who shows us our sins is the forgiving Savior. The One who holds up the high standard is the Almighty who transforms us. The One who diagnoses our soul-sickness and operates on it with our permission is the Great Physician who performs painful surgery on us from time to time for our healing and greater good. The One who asks us to die to our sin and selfishness is the Risen Jesus who loves us more than His own life.

Intimates of God have a realistic view of

their own sinfulness, but they also know the holiness imputed to them through Christ. As a result, these redeemed sinners have been able to testify, as A. W. Tozer did, "I have found God to be cordial and generous and in every way easy to live with."

PART IV

INTEGRATING

UNDERSTANDING

But the man who looks intently into the perfect
law that gives freedom, and continues to do
this, not forgetting what he had heard, but
doing it—he will be blessed in what he does
(James 1:25, NIV).

CHAPTER 10

THINK
THINGS
THROUGH

What we know is important, but what we do with what we know is critical. Nurturing intimacy with God requires more than simply collecting facts about Him and discovering information about ourselves. We must continually integrate what we learn if our knowledge is to be effective and productive.

THE PROBLEM WITH KNOWLEDGE

As I observe it, many in the family of God, in spite of the information they have, live like neglected orphans. Some are crippled by chronic fear, resentment, despondency, low self-esteem, guilt, and worry. Others give in to prejudice, greed, lust, abusiveness, intemperance, denial, and escapism. In short, they bear little of the Family likeness to the Father whom they profess to know and love. They seem to be missing out on the blessings of being in relationship with Him: love, joy, peace, patience, kindness, goodness, faithfulness, gentleness, and self-control (Gal. 5:22 and 23).

For example, when Joe married, his bride was pregnant. He still feels the guilt of his premarital sexual activity. As a result, he's spent his life atoning for his sin against his firstborn by giving him almost anything he's wanted. As the kid hit the teen years, the father reacted to memories of his adolescent dating experience by trying to control his son's life in unrealistic ways. His actions and attitudes toward himself and his child haven't reflected what he says he believes about Jesus Christ.

Judy attended Bible college and then became a minister's wife. She vocally witnessed about her faith in the Lord and claimed He was everything to her. But then her only daughter rebelled, blasphemed Christ, and adopted a destructive lifestyle. Judy went into years of depression from which she never recovered. It seems she was controlled more by her daughter than by the Holy Spirit.

Dave still gets tied up in knots of bitterness

when he remembers how a pastor harshly treated him. Beverly weakly and fearfully refuses to intervene to keep her husband from verbally abusing their children. Ed reads pornographic magazines and feels a lot of self-loathing as a result. Joan perpetually keeps her friends waiting and thoughtlessly wastes their time by arriving late to meetings; though she apologizes for her habitual tardiness, she doesn't change.

All these people are Christians who are sincere about their relationships with God. Some are even engaged in ministry. So why don't they experience and express more of Christ's nature?

Consider three reasons. One, it may be that they just have not understood who God is or the provision He has made for meeting their needs. As a result, they live as if He doesn't have either the resources they sorely need or the will to act on their behalf. Two, perhaps, they simply aren't aware of who they are and how much they fall short of being an attractive witness for Christ. Maybe they don't understand how abundant the abundant life that Christ promised can be; so they think living with their problems is normal. Three, possibly they have a fairly good grasp of the kind of God they belong to and are clear-eyed about who they are, but they either can't or won't relate the two in a way that transforms their lives. This may be due to ignorance of how to appropriate God's resources, unbelief that change is possible for them, or an unwillingness to yield that area of their lives to the Lord.

You see, it's possible to cram our brains full of biblical information which makes no difference in our lives. Facts and ideas may do little more than titillate our intellects and puff us up (1 Cor. 8:1). To know a lot of theology doesn't necessarily ensure that we will apply what we know in practical ways. We can be doctrinally educated far beyond our spiritual experience. That's why people with seminary degrees aren't automatically giants of the faith.

It's also possible to gain insight into who we are and be no further ahead in terms of nurturing intimacy with God. We've probably all run into folks who know details of their childhood and how that's shaped their adult lives, but they don't necessarily benefit from the insight. If understanding oneself inevitably and significantly changed people for the better, then psychotherapy is salvation and the best source of spiritual growth.

Nurturing intimacy with God requires blending what we know of God and ourselves in such a way that we are transformed. This integration is nourished through meditation, faith, and prayer. Let's deal with meditation first.

THE ACTIVITY OF HOLY THOUGHT

To begin with, we should clear away any confusion between Christian meditation and

Eastern meditation right up front. "Eastern meditation is an attempt to empty the mind; Christian meditation is an attempt to fill the mind. . . . Eastern forms of meditation stress the need to become detached from the world. . . There is no God to be attached to or to hear from," explains Richard Foster.[1] The popular transcendental meditation offers folks the happiness and peace of an empty mind through a meditation-produced state of altered consciousness. This is *not* the kind of meditation that the Bible talks about. When teachers of spirituality recommend a practice which promotes emptying the self of all concepts, thought, and sensation, they are not advocating a Christian practice.

A concern about Eastern religious activity should not cause believers to shy away from meditation. Scripture commands it. The Israelites were told to meditate day and night on the law the Lord God Almighty had given them (Josh. 1:8). David said the godly person is the one who delights in the law and meditates on it day and night (Ps. 1:2). When Asaph felt disturbed because the wicked seem to prosper while the righteous are plagued on every side, he saw that his thinking was foolish after he spent time meditating in the sanctuary (Ps. 73). These passages indicate that godly meditation focuses one's thoughts on and contemplates God, His Word, and His works. Expanding on this definition, J. I. Packer wrote:

> Meditation is the activity of calling to mind, and thinking over, and dwelling on, and applying to oneself, the various things that one knows about the works and ways and purposes and promises of God. It is an activity of holy thought, consciously performed in the presence of God, under the eye of God, by the help of God, as a means of communion with God. Its purpose is to clear one's mental and spiritual vision of God, and to let His truth make its full and proper impact on one's mind and heart. It's a matter of talking to oneself; it is, indeed, often a matter of arguing with oneself, reasoning oneself out of moods of doubt and unbelief into a clear apprehension of God's power and grace.[2]

Through meditation we are able personally and practically to relate and apply what we know of God to what we know of ourselves and our condition. By this means, our information results in the formation of a deeper relationship between the Lord and us. What does this look like in an everyday situation?

One weekend, I flew to a city and addressed 500 women at a retreat. I talked to them about exercising faith in God in ways that would make a positive, practical change in their lives. I counseled with some who were dealing with confusion, guilt, grief, lust, a sense of inadequacy. People expressed appreciation for my ministry; they were generous in their compliments.

As I returned home, there, 35,000 feet in the air, I didn't have a great feeling of satisfaction. I knew how folks often hear truth and manage to ignore it. I also knew how conferences often result in a temporary emotional high which amounts to little in terms of spiritual growth in their lives. I wondered if the sacrifice of three days away from my husband and home was worth it. Had my expenditure of time and energy made any real difference? By the time I arrived home, I realized that I was feeling somewhat depressed.

I wrote down all my concerns in my journal and noted that I was physically drained by jet lag, talking with hurting women late into the night, and having had to sleep—or try to—in a strange bed for two nights. I acknowledged my great desire to make my life count, to make a good contribution to the kingdom of God. I admitted that I hated to think my efforts may have amounted to little or nothing. I confessed that I enjoyed hearing of fantastic results—like receiving a letter a year later from a woman who says her life was radically transformed by what she heard at the retreat. I was also aware of the fact that the enemy of my soul was urging me to accept his lies and destroy my confidence in Christ. Without a doubt, I was in touch with who I was and what was going on inside me.

Then I got a good night's sleep in my own bed. I was amazed to see once again how a spiritual problem doesn't seem to be so big when I'm physically rested. Yet, some nagging questions lingered about the effectiveness of my ministry.

Rather than bouncing out of bed the next morning, I lay there and meditated on who the Lord is. The good Shepherd cares far more for His sheep than do I, His underling; He's responsible for their nourishment and growth. He's promised that His Word doesn't return void but accomplishes what He purposes. I remembered His exhortation not to be weary in well doing for at the right time there'll be a harvest to reap (Gal. 6:9). I recalled His command: "Be steadfast, immovable, always abounding in the work of the Lord, knowing that your labor is not in vain in the Lord" (1 Cor. 15:58). I pondered the fact that the requirement for those who have been entrusted with a ministry is faithfulness (1 Cor. 4:2).

Later as I poured myself a cup of coffee, I regained confidence to continue serving God and His people as I have the opportunity. I was comforted by knowing in my deep-down-inside self that I can minister in the power of the Holy Spirit and leave the results to God. I don't need to see the full results of my work; I only need to be faithful and to trust His faithfulness.

Obviously, this "calling to mind, and thinking over, and dwelling on, and applying to oneself, the various things that one knows about the works and ways and purposes and promises of God," as Packer so aptly describes meditation, indicates the primary part the mind plays in developing a relationship with the Lord. The greatest commandment speaks of loving the Lord our God with all our mind (Luke 10:27). As Richard C. Raines noted, "It does not take a great mind to be a Christian, but it takes all the mind a man [or woman] has."

A TIME TO BE STILL

Directing our minds to ponder the mind of Christ requires time and quietness. For that reason, God says, "Be still, and know that I am God" (Ps. 46:10). But hushing in the hustle of life is not as easy as it may appear. A body in motion tends to remain in motion, and our society gives movers and shakers a lot of affirmation. As a result, hyperactive types, who plan full days of productivity, often feel as if they are wasting time—especially when work is demanding their attention—by pausing to gain God's perspective on life. Even Christians get perplexed as to why Jesus would leave an effective evangelistic campaign and go off to pray: Isn't sharing the good news more important than restoring one's soul (Luke 5:15–16)? Other people resist quiet time because they are afraid of silence. They are scared of what they may discover in the quiet of their hearts. Consequently, they turn on the radio the minute they get in the car or the television as soon as they walk through the door of their house. They depend on muzak, constant chatter, or busyness to keep the threatening silence at a distance. To be still represents a risk of the highest order to the tenuous emotional equilibrium they've built on denial.

Before you and I will take time for meditation, we must be convinced that our relationship with God is a pearl of great price, that contemplation is some of the best work that we can do. Every other activity in which we may engage is wood, hay, and stubble by comparison. We must also believe that the truth never hurts us as much as ignorance or lies do, and that the pain of facing a problem is not as excruciating as the ache of neglecting to deal with it. We must be convinced that burying distressing facts can destroy us; baring them before God will not.

Taking time for quietness in the presence of our loving Abba is crucial because He gets missed by those who expect Him to announce His arrival with a trumpet blast. If He speaks always in wind, earthquake, and fire, then we need not be still; we will hear Him over the roar of full schedules. But if He whispers, then we must be silent to catch His message (1 Kings 19:11,12). Speaking in a soft voice, He easily gets drowned out by radio and television (even the Christian variety), phone calls, business dealings, shopping, social activities, church meetings, and even good works. Understanding this, we realize the value of giving deliberate, uninterrupted attention to our relationship with our Bridegroom in order to nurture our intimacy with Him. "The detachment from the confusion all around us is in order to have a richer attachment to God."[3]

This does not necessarily mean, however, that all productive quiet time always requires the cessation of all other activity. Consider the two on the road to Emmaus. As they walked home softly talking together and processing what they had just experienced in Jerusalem, Jesus came alongside. He met them as they walked and talked, and their hearts burned within them; but they were dull to the reality of His presence. Only when He broke bread with them did they realize they were with the risen Christ (Luke 24:13–32). Had they been open to the possibility, they may have recognized Him on the pathway of their journey.

Some activities do not demand much conscious concentration and, therefore, leave the mind free to consider Christ. We can be engaged in "talking to oneself . . . arguing with oneself, reasoning oneself out of moods of doubt and unbelief into a clear apprehension of God's power and grace" while doing all kinds of things. I have thought deep thoughts while ironing, washing dishes, and preparing dinner. With my hands meaningfully employed, I have made silent commitments and resolutions, recognized and confessed a sin, adored the Father for His goodness, recalled His promises and benefits, and appropriated His gifts. I have wonderful talks with my Abba when I'm driving the car, waiting in doctors' offices, riding in airplanes.

The point is that every person has "a train of thought on which he [or she] rides when . . . alone," as Joseph Newton said. And we can be alone in a crowd; we can meet Him in the privacy of our souls though surrounded by people. We can take advantage of various situations to ride our train of thought into a conscious sense of connecting with God.

Consistently, however, meditation should involve stopping all other activity and being quiet, because love relationships want and need times of concentrating-on-each-other aloneness. We need the secret prayer closet Jesus mentioned. But we may also take advantage of opportunities in the ordinary routine of life to engage in reflection, routine activities that involve our bodies but leave our minds free to contemplate our Father.

What is the outcome of meditation? It's important to understand that contemplation seldom results in receiving each day some great revelation that makes for a fast, dramatic change in us. To try to tally the assets of our quiet time daily probably won't yield an impressive bottom line in our spiritual account. We normally won't make a killing in the heavenly market in a 24-hour period.

Daily reflection on Truth, however, prepares the soil, plants a seed, covers it over to germinate in the darkness, warms it, waters it, weeds, and cultivates it. As the months and years roll by, the seed of a thought produces fruit—a slow, dramatic change in us. In our periods of meditation, we enter into intimate moments with our Bridegroom and draw near to His heart. Increasingly we find ourselves thinking His thoughts, caring about what He cares about, willing His will, and doing what He commands. We are taking on the Family traits.

CHAPTER 11

BELIEVE IT'S TRUE

Faith, along with meditation and prayer, is one of the essentials for integrating what we know of God with what we know of ourselves. Our relationships of authentic intimacy have a large measure of trust between us and the other person involved. The level of mutual confidence has a direct bearing on the depth of our friendships. Trust enables us to function in our relationship with God and with people.

I never saw a more poignant example of trust than I witnessed in 1988 when my husband had a camp assignment through the Christian youth ministry that he worked for at the time.

During the two weeks we were at that wonderful northern California property, I met Bob.

When I first saw him, he held a white cane and was being led to a meeting by one of his counselors. I remember wondering if he would have any fun at camp and if he would be able to participate in the crazy activities it offered. I soon realized that Bob's blindness didn't seem to slow him down; he entered into almost everything that happened. He even drove a go-cart.

In spite of that, I had my doubts about whether he could do the ropes course. This activity has teenagers walk on logs and cables 20 feet above the ground. At the end, they have to climb a ladder to a platform about 40 feet up in the air. From there, they jump for a trapeze bar. If they miss it or fall at any point on the course, they won't be hurt because they're securely roped into a safety system. I couldn't believe it when I saw Bob walk the ropes course better than 95 percent of all campers and then leap through the air for the bar.

How could he do that? I think it was because he'd had to trust folks to be his eyes and do exactly as they said, or he'd have been limited all his young life. Unlike most of his sighted peers, he had learned to obey quickly, so that's the way he responded to the instructions of his ropes-course guides. He had to believe that they weren't endangering his life and that they wanted to help him be successful. To do as others asked had always required of Bob a certain level of faith that they meant him good and not harm.

WE INVEST FAITH

As I watched Bob that bright July afternoon, I was reminded of Jesus' message that people are blessed when they don't see and yet believe, as He had said to Thomas who had not accepted the other disciples' reports of His resurrection (John 20:29). The doubter had declared that he'd believe only if he could touch the wounds of His nail-pierced hands and speared side.

If we had been in Thomas' sandals, would we have responded differently? Consider how unbelieving believers can be. They can worry themselves sick about situations over which they have no control. They can try to fix people whom only God can change. They can excuse their destructive angry outbursts by saying they were born with a hot temper and can't do anything about it. They can hold on to bitterness over offenses committed against them. They can love things and use people in an attempt to gain a sense of worth or power. They can go around feeling guilty though they've confessed their sins. They can beg God for what He's already given. In essence, believers don't always believe their heavenly Father is the wise, powerful, forgiving, loving, transforming, generous, sovereign One the Scriptures reveal.

This is sad because the extent to which believers don't believe is a major factor in destroying their sense of connection with God. They know the truth in their heads; they may even teach and preach it. But they don't personally, actively respond to it in a way that draws them nearer the Savior. That's why Hebrews 11:6 says that it's impossible to please God without faith. Thus, it's foolish even to imagine that we can have a delightful, intimate relationship with Him and not trust Him and take Him at His word. Totally. Implicitly.

Some folks lament that they don't have faith. That's simply not so. We all have faith, and we exercise it every day. We drop a check in the mail to pay the mortgage and trust the postal system to deliver it to the finance company. We pump fuel into our automobiles and trust that it is gasoline and not high-priced water. We take medicine the doctor prescribes only because we are confident that it will benefit and not harm us. We fly in airplanes because we believe they will get us to our destination safely. Yes, we have faith and often invest incredible amounts of it in people we don't even know. We have to. We trust that the one who stands at the altar beside us loves us and will be good to us, so we make vows of fidelity until death parts us. We invest in our children because we trust that our care for and training of them will result in responsible adults. We share secrets with friends because we trust their discretion and loyalty. We couldn't survive in our society without trust.

God asks us to take the capacity we have to trust and have faith in Him. So, we study Scripture and learn who He is and who we are and what He wants us to be about. Through meditation we wrestle with what that truth means and how it relates and applies to us in personal and practical ways. Then we must go a step further if that truth is to be effective and productive; we must respond to it in faith.

Our Abba tells us the attributes of His glorious character, and He expects us to believe that what He's told us about Himself is true simply because He said so. He doesn't ask us to comprehend why and how, but to trust that He acts consistently with His revelation. As Oswald Chambers wrote, "Faith is not intelligent understanding; faith is deliberate commitment to a Person where I see no way."[1]

The Lord also tells us about ourselves: He says we are sinners, fall short of His glory, and deserve the death sentence for our crimes against Him; but we can be forgiven through Jesus Christ. He says we can also forgive others who have deeply wounded us, experience victory over temptation and sin, and see real change in our life so that we act more like Christ. We can know His joy and peace. He assures us that we are His children and heirs, and we possess all we need for life and godliness. We are chosen, royal, holy. We will one day be with Him eternally in the home He's prepared for us. These are the facts. Again, we need not perfectly understand the why and how in all of this.

The important issue is that we have to make a decision about whether or not we will accept our Father's evaluation of us, our position, and our condition. Will we believe all He has said without seeing the evidence first? To grow in our relationship with Him, it's absolutely crucial that we trust what He's said He's done to meet us where we are.

FAITH PAYS HEALTHY DIVIDENDS

As I've mentioned earlier, I gave mental assent to the fact that God is love years before I realized it in my life in a practical way. One day the truth that God loves everybody became personal: Nothing can separate *me* from the love of God (Rom. 8:38–39). He loves *me* with eternal love (Jer. 31:3). His goodness and mercy follow *me* all the days of my life (Ps. 23:6). Yes, Jesus loves the world, but He also loves me, the individual, and my faith-response requires that I know that on an intensely personal level.

I admit that some days I don't feel my Bridegroom's love or see how some circumstances He permits in my life express His care.

But as Chambers said, "Faith is not a pathetic sentiment, but robust, vigorous confidence built on the fact that God is holy love. You cannot see Him just now, you cannot understand what He is doing, but you know *Him*."[2]

Because I trust Him, even on those days when I don't feel cherished, I accept the reality that my Abba's allowances are somehow good for me. When I choose to count on His love, I open myself to experience a sense of security and significance that doubt would make elusive. I identify with Andrew Murray's statement: "I have seen what has been written concerning me in God's book; I have seen the image of what I am called in God's counsel to be: this thought inspires the soul with a faith that conquers the world."[3]

James put it well when he said that faith works. What we believe will inevitably reveal itself in our words, actions, and attitudes. Faith either influences and affects who we are, or it is weak, nonexistent, or dead (James 2:17–18). That means then, if we believers believe what we say is true, faith motivates our actions as we relate to the daily situations we face. For example, faith in God's forgiveness helps us reject feelings of guilt for confessed sins. Trust in His sovereignty brings us comfort because we know that He is in control of our circumstances no matter how painful or confusing they are to us. Belief in His abiding, constant presence reassures us when we feel all alone. Trust in His overcoming power encourages us when we confront the frustration of besetting sins.

Jonna (not her real name) understands this. A while back she came to me for counseling. As we talked, I discovered that Jonna was reeling because she'd been unfaithful to her husband. As a longtime Christian, she felt guilt, self-loathing, shame, and confusion. She blamed her husband for not being loving enough. Since she had asked her pastor for premarital counsel, she laid some fault on him for not advising her against the marriage. She also held God responsible because He hadn't prevented her wedding to a man who turned out to be different than what she had hoped for, wanted, and needed. She expressed so much anger at God, her husband, her situation, and—most of all—herself that I felt she probably disliked me as well. She seemed to test me and my ability to accept her, and I wondered if I would pass. But you know the saying—any old port in a storm. So, desperate, she reached out to me hoping I could help.

After Jonna had spilled out hurt, resentment, and frustration, she asked what advice I could give her. You may have counseled her in a different vein, perhaps pointed out the immorality of her behavior and her sinful attitude. Jonna, however, was very much aware of all that. I simply told her she needed to trust God as He is. I encouraged her to take what she'd learned about Him during her childhood in church and stake her very life on its truth. Before she would ever experience His rest, she had to believe in God's love, forgiveness, sovereignty, wisdom, and power as being personally applicable to her and her situation.

I said to her, "This may sound simplistic to a bright, well-educated woman, but the only thing I have to offer you is what I've based my life on. I choose to believe that regardless of the mess I find myself in, God is indeed my wonderful Counselor, my mighty God, and my eternal Father (Isa. 9:6). When I trust His wisdom, power, and love, I've found Him to be my Prince of Peace. You can accept this or reject this, but I don't have anything else to offer you."

This sounded elementary to me as I spoke it that day. It *is* elementary. We either believe God is who He has revealed Himself to be, or we sense a distance in our relationship with Him. Trust is an intrinsic aspect of our intimacy with Him.

My advice made sense to Jonna. She made a choice to have faith in the Lord as the Bible reveals Him and not as she felt He might be. She believed she was forgiven and loved, and God began to heal her. Later she wrote to me:

> Isaiah 9:6 has become my focal point. When the truth about God's sovereignty broke through the walls I'd built around my heart, it seemed as if a dam had broken inside me.

It's been day after day of identifying and committing more and more of myself to my Father. It hasn't been easy, but it's been a peaceful process.

He's causing me to have life, full of an awareness of His control and my dependence on Him. He is enough. If all else fails, if no one loves me, if no one needs me, if my life goes by in a seemingly boring way, if I never reach my potential, if I never am used of God in ministry, if loneliness becomes my companion, He is enough.

My daily quiet times with my Father have been leisurely, prayerful, loving times of reflection, study, prayer, journaling, and praise. God has taken a lover, and it is me!

When I met Jonna, she had just learned some shocking things about herself. She had never known she was capable of committing the sins she had. Her self-respect was shattered. She realized that she was weak and that scared her. Stripped of her former self-assurance, she wondered if she would fall into sin again even though she knew to do so would jeopardize her relationship with her family and destroy her ministry.

Jonna began to place what she had known about God since her childhood alongside her new self-awareness. Because of her years of Christian education, I really didn't have to tell her much about Him that she had not already read or heard in her Bible-preaching church.

Jonna's problem was that she was not integrating what she knew of God and what she knew of herself. She hadn't seen the implications of truth and then appropriated that by faith to the circumstances in which she found herself. She didn't believe in her heart what she knew in her head. She didn't exercise the trust that made information experience. When she did, she came to sense an overwhelming, satisfying intimacy with Jesus Christ.

That's understandable if we accept what A. W. Thorold said, "The highest pinnacle of the spiritual life is not joy in unbroken sunshine, but absolute and undoubting trust in the love of God." That's authentic intimacy—unshakable fidelity to the Lover of our souls.

CHAPTER 12

PRAYER THAT TRANS- FORMS

*T*o integrate our increasing knowledge of God and self, so that our spiritual relationship grows, requires prayer as well as meditation and faith. As Jesus walked in the flesh on earth, He experienced intimacy with God the Father, and we will know that intimacy also if we make prayer a way of life as He did.

"How much prayer meant to Jesus! . . . When perplexed he prayed. When hard pressed by work he prayed. When hungry for fellowship he found it in prayer. He chose his associates and received his messages upon his knees. If tempted, he prayed. If criticized, he prayed. If fatigued in body or wearied in spirit, he had recourse to his one unfailing habit of prayer," wrote S. D. Gordon in *Quiet Talks on Prayer*. In Gethsemane He prayed; He poured out His anguish, asked for the cup to pass, received His Father's answer, and yielded to His will.

For Jesus, praying was an attitude as much as an action; it expressed His moment-by-moment fellowship with His Father. It didn't seem to be a duty to Him. His ministry was so crucial and busy that apparently He thought He could not afford *not* to pray.

WHAT IS PRAYER?

What is prayer? Commonly understood, prayer is communication between God and one of His followers. It is the communion of two of us who love each other. It is our wanting to share with our Beloved all our thoughts, feelings, hopes, desires, hurts, confusions—our entire selves. It is our longing to hear, in an intensely personal way, our Bridegroom express His heart and will on specific matters.

Prayer can be like the mundane conversations essential to people in a relationship—like asking a family member to bring home a loaf of French bread for dinner. It may be like a shopping list of things needed, a laundry list of things to be cleaned up, a thank-you-note list of things to express appreciation for.

Our exclamations of praise, anger, joy, fear, love, hate, gratitude—the gamut of human emotions—may be a means of communicating our inner being to God and inviting His response. Prayer can be spoke in body language—tears, laughter, sighs, applause and even rest—when we recognize that He is indeed present with us and for us at any time, in any place, in any situation. Some prayers we set to music; we sing them: "Holy, holy, holy, Lord God Almighty" expresses our adoration. "Draw me nearer, nearer, nearer, blessed Lord" verbalizes our longing to be closer to Him.

WHY SHOULD WE PRAY?

Why is prayer important in nurturing intimacy with God? When we meditate, we contemplate truth and personally apply it. When we trust, we stake our lives on truth and choose to act on it. When we pray, we verbally express to God our acceptance of and accountability for the truth we profess we know and trust. Our words make the abstract concrete: this is truly what we think and believe. When we voice our worship, we declare our conviction of His worth. When we direct adoration to Him, we indicate our appreciation of His person. Our praise acknowledges Him as the Giver of our gifts. Our petitions reveal our neediness and our awareness that He wants to and can help. Our confession of sins proves we realize that our transgressions are against Him and our expectation that He is forgiving.

Kenneth Swanson wrote, "From a biblical perspective, the motive for prayer is to enter the Kingdom of God, a kingdom that is defined solely in terms of intimacy with God. Human beings were created to live in that intimacy. Why do we pray? Prayer is the doorway to that Kingdom."[1]

The parent knows what the child needs and wants but still appreciates the confidence the child shows by asking. The wife knows she's loved, but she relishes her husband's verbalizing his feelings. In some ways, to ask why we need to pray is to question the value of communicating with any person close to us—parent, spouse, child, or friend. Common sense tells us that whatever form our conversations with God take, prayer is imperative to a healthy, growing relationship with Him. In fact, the level of communication indicates the degree of our spiritual intimacy.

WHEN DO WE PRAY?

Brother Lawrence noted,

The most holy practice, the nearest to daily life, and the most essential for the spiritual life, is the practice of the presence of God, that is to find joy in his divine company and to make it a habit of life, speaking humbly and conversing lovingly with him at all times, every moment, without rule or restriction, above all at times of temptation, distress, dryness, and revulsion, and even of faithlessness and sin.

We address and listen to God when we gather as a group of His people to worship and learn. Individually, we speak and listen to God all day long. That's a bit of what it means to pray without ceasing. We pray for the one we're dialing on the phone—or when we're put on hold. We thank our Creator for the beautiful day when we see the sunshine or rain He sends. We talk to Him about the stress of our schedule when our plans are interrupted by unplanned events. We ask His wisdom as we are about to meet with a friend. We seek His guidance for a decision we're asked to make. We claim His promises when we need His resources. We know He is with us, and we consciously include Him in the routine of our day.

At the same time, the closest relationships always require private, do-not-disturb, let's-focus-intensely-on-each-other times. Quality friendships need more than hit-and-run conversations if they are to deepen. If we cherish and long to nurture our relationship with God, we will set time aside to stop in the madness of the too-much-with-us world, with its assault on every sense, in order to fix attention on, seek expression of, and open ourselves up to the experience of intimate communion in spirit and truth.

The more frequently and consistently we pray in the closet (Matt. 6:6), the stronger the intimacy becomes. As Andrew Murray wrote, "The law of the manna, that what is heavenly cannot remain good long upon earth, but must day by day be renewed afresh from heaven, still holds good."[2] Mitch Finley said it succinctly, "Without daily private prayer, Christians face spiritual anorexia."

HOW DO WE PRAY?

When I first began to pray as a child, I didn't give much thought about how to do it. I had a heavenly Father, and I wanted and needed to talk to Him. I took great delight in praying, "Now I lay me down to sleep. . . ." I asked God to bless everyone. With folded hands I thanked Him for food. I prayed for forgiveness of sins and asked Him to come into my five-year-old heart. As I gasped for air when I had asthma, I asked Him to help me breathe and grant me healing. Later I beseeched Him for the salvation of loved ones and help in being good. I told Him I would serve Him with my life. I asked His direction in decisions. When in trouble, my first instinct was like that of Peter, who yelled as he began to sink beneath the waves, "Lord, save me!" (Matt. 14:30). It was all so simple— as natural as talking to my family or friends.

Somewhere along the line, however, prayer became complicated. Maybe it's because I began hearing lots about the discipline of prayer. How hard it is to pray. How none of us do enough of it. How the world is going to perdition on skis because we aren't persistent in intercession. How conversational prayer is *the* relevant manner for the 20th century. How important it is to address the correct person of the Trinity. How ACTS (adoration, confession, thanksgiving, and supplication) is the best formula. How ACTS is all right, but the Lord's Prayer recited daily is crucial. How saying the Jesus Prayer (Mark 10:47) for twenty minutes each day makes saints of sinners. How what we really need is just to be in the presence of Jesus and say nothing at all.

Along the way, I began to lose the ease of praying I had had in childhood. Part of me says that's fine; when I became an adult I should have put away childish things. Another part of me remembers that Jesus said we must all be as little children of our Abba. As Mother Teresa said, "Prayer is quite simple. We must not complicate matters. When Jesus was asked by his disciples, 'Master, teach us to pray,' he answered, 'You will pray like this, Our Father. . . .' He did not teach them any methods or techniques.

He said simply that we should speak to God as to our Father, a loving Father."[3]

Part of me thinks prayer should be like conversation with a good friend, with the kind of openness Dinah Maria Mulock Craik describes between friends: "Oh, the comfort, the inexpressible comfort of feeling safe with a person. Having neither to weigh thoughts, nor measure words, but pouring them all out, just as they are, chaff and grain together, certain that a faithful hand will take and sift them, keep what is worth keeping, and with a breath of kindness blow the rest away." If God is our Friend who loves us infinitely and unconditionally, do we need to weigh thoughts and measure words with Him? Pray in formulas? Consider time amounts?

Do we need to use words all the time? Isn't a mark of intimacy with friends the way they can be together in comfortable silence? Andrew Murray wrote of this aspect of prayer, "Let the principal part of my prayer be the holy silence and adoration of faith, in which I wait upon God, until He reveals Himself to me, and gives me, through His Spirit, the loving assurance that He looks down upon me as a Father, that I am well pleasing to Him. He who in prayer has no time in quietness of soul, and in full consciousness of its meaning, to say Abba Father, has missed the best part of prayer."[4]

Having said all this, a part of me also realizes that God is far more than our good buddy.

He's our holy and majestic King. Our relationship with Him is not one of equals. He's the superior with whom we inferiors must deal. Dare we inconsiderately keep rushing pell-mell into His royal presence? The wise man of Ecclesiastes had a good point when he wrote, "Do not be rash with your mouth, and let not your heart utter anything hastily before God. For God is in heaven, and you are on earth; therefore let your words be few" (5:2). Few words show simplicity, humility, faith—characteristics consistent with godly living.

On the one hand, we converse easily and openly with those we love; on the other, we find that communication is hard work no matter how strong and mature our friendship is with another. To speak the truth lovingly (Eph. 4:15) and listen quickly (James 1:19) are skills we have to learn and practice. To know when and how to speak up and to listen demands careful thought.

LEARNING TO PRAY

Since effective communication requires education of both the classroom and the laboratory variety, it makes sense that you and I can improve our communion with God by listening to sermons and reading books on prayer. We should keep in mind, however, that the Father loves to hear from us, His children, even if we speak with lisp, stammer, or poor structure. We pray the best way we know how and don't let doubts about not knowing how interfere. We realize that we mature spiritually and in our praying with time and experience.

When I was in my twenties, I remember asking God for something that I knew was good and proper to pray for. Yet as I made my petition over what seemed a long period of time, nothing seemed to happen. I wasn't getting what I was praying for. In the process of bringing my request to Him daily, however, I became open to hear some things He said to me. He let me know that, while my request was fine, my motives were out of line. Pride was at the root of my petition. I confessed my sin, accepted His forgiveness, and experienced a new sense of closeness to the Lord as a result.

I've found a request offered over an extended period of time does change with the repeated asking because God adds His wisdom and insight to bring the request into line with His will and to purify the asker. Often, like the prodigal son, we may find ourselves beginning with *give me* and ending up with *make me* (Luke 15:11–32). If prayer does not change us, perhaps we are not engaging in dialogue with God but only monologue. Maybe we are arrogantly assuming our petitions are proper; therefore, we don't question the possibility that they may be out of line. Surely this is the reason for a persistently carnal pray-er. Real communication is not only talking but listening and being willing to be changed by what we hear.

If we practice authentic prayer, we will grow to be like Christ. We will communicate with the Father, as Jesus did, on the basis of our knowledge of His character and purpose, which is to glorify the Son. We will gain sensitivity to know what to ask. After years of abiding in Christ, we will become clearer about His will and pray in His name. As a result, we will, as the writer of Hebrews said, "come boldly to the throne of grace" (4:16).

No matter how mature we become in faith, how purified our desires, or how content in Christ, we remain children dependent on the Father for eternal life, love, joy, peace, patience, goodness, faithfulness, temperance, and all other Christlike qualities as well as guidance, food, shelter, health, employment, and more. Our prayers acknowledge our need, and we never cease to be needy.

We don't pray primarily, however, to order items from God's warehouse any more than friends talk primarily to get something from each other. Friends converse to cultivate their relationship; we pray to nurture our relationship with our Friend. As Mother Teresa said, "Prayer enlarges the heart until it is capable of containing God's gift of Himself." At the same time, prayer is a means of giving ourselves to Him.

No matter how deep our relationship with

our Abba grows, we will never think our communication with Him comes close to approaching
perfection. I know I still walk cautiously as I
try to balance my praying between the childish
and the childlike. I don't want to be childishly
selfish, whining, demanding; at the same time,
I do desire to have a child's unquestioning trust
in a loving Father as I try to integrate what I'm
learning of Him with what I understand of what
I am, want, think, do, feel.

Most of all, as C. S. Lewis wrote, I desire
this in my communication with God: "May it
be the real I who speaks. May it be the real Thou
that I speak to."[5]

PART V

REALIZING

UNDERSTANDING

Just as you are in me and I am in you, so they
will be in us, and the world will believe you
sent me (John 17:21 LB).

CHAPTER 13

SHARE
THE
LOVE

When we've wholeheartedly given ourselves to the venture of nurturing intimacy with God, we'll discover that our relationship is not just Jesus and me in a tight little twosome. There's no room in this venture for exclusivity. As Nicholas Wolterstorff wrote, "It seems to me that the Christian life, when properly lived, is a rhythmic alternation between turning toward God in worship and running toward the world in love, . . . between congregation and dispersal, liturgy and labor, worship and work, adoration and obedience."[1]

Thinking about this reminds me of an old

gospel song I used to hear a lot that went something like this: "On the Jericho Road, there's room for just two—no more or no less—just Jesus and you." The lyrics paint a cozy picture and make, I suppose, a valid point. On the other hand, they give me the uneasy feeling I got when I saw a car with a bumper sticker that read, "Welcome to Colorado. Now go home." That driver wanted to let folks know that he'd prefer to keep all this state's magnificent scenery and quality of life just for those of us who already live here. Maybe Colorado does have a limited capacity, but the Jericho Road does not.

Perhaps, however, we all have a little bit of Peter in us. When we feel good about our relationship with God and experience a spiritual high, as the apostle did when he witnessed the Transfiguration, we're prone to say, "Rabbi, it is good for us to be here; and let us make three tabernacles: one for You, one for Moses, and one for Elijah" (Mark 9:5). In other words, "Can't we pitch tents and camp out here? If people need anything, let them come to us." We want to remain on a mountaintop with major advantages and minor disturbances in our lives.

The next verse notes that, though he spoke, Peter really didn't know what to say. And when we are tempted to retreat from everyday life in an effort to seek or preserve a certain spiritual experience, we don't know what we're asking for either.

I understand why Peter and we desire to live on the mountain with only Jesus there. Jesus, however, led His three friends back down into the valley, where they immediately confronted grim reality: a demonized man who desperately needed help. Our Lord will always take His intimates into the ordinariness of their world—into job, school, market, home—to meet the real needs of real people.

THE HALLMARK OF GOD'S INTIMATES

In drawing nearer to the Lord, we realize that, though we are indeed pilgrims and strangers in this world, God asks us to stay in our world as active, vital witnesses to those for whom He gave His life. So we regularly withdraw to a private place to nurture our love relationship with God, just as Jesus frequently did; and then, with a renewed conviction and comfort in that intimacy with Him, we go back out into the public arena. That's because "The only thing that counts is faith expressing itself through love" (Gal. 5:6, NIV).

Jesus is our example. He walked in perfect harmony with His Father, and He showed more love to both the masses and the individual than anybody who has ever walked this Earth. Because He was full of compassion, He fed the hungry, healed the sick, raised the dead, taught the spiritually ignorant, and asked prayer for helpers to reap a spiritual harvest. He explained His actions this way: "My Father has been working until now, and I have been working" (John 5:17). The Father and the Son willed one will, and the result was Jesus' ministry to people.

A devoted relationship with God always manifests itself in love for others. In fact, the whole of salvation history reveals God's extending Himself in love to people. Consequently, it's inconceivable that when we walk intimately with Him that we will do otherwise. Because our Father is always working, we, too, will work. His nature is to reach out to others in love, and we share that nature. Oscar Hammerstein II, whether he knew it or not, expressed good theology when he wrote, "And love in the heart wasn't put there to stay;/Love isn't love 'till you give it away." Love is the hallmark of Christ's followers. As He said, "By this all will know that you are My disciples, if you have love for one another" (John 13:35).

Henry Drummond wrote, "We have been . . . told that the greatest thing in the religious world is faith. . . . If we have been told that, we may miss the mark. In the thirteenth chapter of 1 Corinthians, Paul takes us to Christianity at its source: and there we see, 'The greatest of these is love.' "[2]

Paul told the Roman church, "Love is the fulfillment of the law" (Rom. 13:10). That says that when we truly love, we find that we are effectively obeying the commandments of Scripture. No wonder, then, Peter wrote, *"Above all things,* have fervent love for one another" (1 Pet. 4:8, italics mine).

John wrote in his first epistle, "God is love" (4:8). The sign of our intimacy with our loving Father, Husband, and Friend is our being loving people. Show me an unloving person, and I will show you one who has not connected with Christ—no matter how much religious activity he or she may be involved in. Our spirituality is not revealed in how much we read the Bible, go to church, or do acts of service. Love is *the* inevitable proof that we have spent a quantity of quality time with Jesus.

The world knows a lot about *luv,* the kind of emotion of popular music, romance novels, and movie plots. It knows little about genuine love. So we must explain what we mean when we say that love is the result of our intimacy with God.

WHAT LOVE LOOKS LIKE

One of the problems in defining love is that we use the word so broadly. We may say we love frozen yogurt (especially of the chocolate mint variety!), alpine meadows with their tiny flowers, the color blue, and our children. This overuse of a good word connected to widely diverse objects of unequal value makes it almost meaningless.

When the New Testament talks about God's love for us, it uses the term *agape*. We understand this as unconditional love or, as C. S. Lewis called it, Divine Gift-love. Agape is love without ifs, whens, or becauses. It's loving freely as God loves; it takes the initiative, accepts, forgives, and sacrifices even to the point of laying down one's life. It applies, as Lewis says, even to those who are not naturally lovable, perhaps even naturally repugnant.

To understand the kind of loving person you and I will become as we experience His agape in our intimate relationship with Him, we need look no further than 1 Corinthians 13. This premier description of agape, penned by Paul, has inspired, challenged, convicted, motivated, and encouraged people through the centuries. It cuts across the sentimental and trite ways most of us think of love. It tells us that speaking in tongues, golden oratory, knowledge, miracles, faith, and service are nothing apart from love. Love is the key ingredient that gives all spiritual exercises, gifts, and ministries meaning.

When we are intimate with Christ, we will find that we are increasingly characterized by this: "Love is patient, love is kind. It does not envy, it does not boast, it is not proud. It is not rude, it is not self-seeking, it is not easily angered, it keeps no record of wrongs. Love does not delight in evil but rejoices with the truth.

It always protects, always trusts, always hopes, always perseveres" (1 Cor. 13:4–8, NIV). Now let's bring this down to where we live.

Paul says love is patient. It handles delays and waits graciously. If we love, we allow people time to grow; and if they never change in positive ways, we endure their imperfections with calmness. We are longsuffering—we can take the suffering others inflict as long as we need to.[3] Our example is God's patience with us in our imperfections and slowness to mature.

Love also is kind. Thus, we do caring deeds for others. We think, speak, and behave in helpful, solicitous ways. We give encouragement, affirmation, practical aid, and relief. When we show kindness to others, Christ accepts those acts as being done for Him (Matt. 25:40). That's a primary way to express our love for the Lover of our souls.

Love doesn't envy. When we care for others, we can't possibly resent them for having good things we don't have. We're happy for the gifts, talents, respect, relationships, recognition, or whatever—even ministry opportunities—that come their way. On the other hand, love doesn't boast. We aren't proud of our gifts, talents, respect, relationships, recognition or whatever that come our way because we know where such blessings originate—God. Humble gratitude is a measure of our love for our Abba who delights in providing His children with good things.

Love isn't rude either. If we love, we'll

have good manners even if we've never read Emily Post or Miss Manners. I'm not talking about stilted "company" manners, but we'll behave graciously and politely as people who care about and respect others. This grows out of the fact that love isn't self-seeking. We aren't selfish people who give higher priority to our wishes, our rights, our ideas, our plans, and our comfort than we do to anybody else's. Since our Husband doesn't force His will on us, we won't be pushy either—even about our spiritual insights. Putting others first is at the heart of etiquette.

Love is not easily angered or provoked. When we love, we're even-tempered. Our relationship with the Prince of Peace allows the fruit of peace to grow in us so that we're not easily disturbed by inconvenience, unkindness, criticism, rudeness. Oh, we still care passionately about justice or get angry at evil, but even then we express that concern in godly ways.

Love keeps no records of wrongs; it throws away the tally sheet. That means we don't mentally rehearse other's sins again and again. We forgive just as God for Christ's sake forgave us—not because pardon is earned or deserved. We don't delight in evil even when it happens to somebody who has hurt us badly. We wish them well.

Love always protects the reputation and person of others. It trusts God's sovereignty over us and everybody who touches us; we're in His care. It hopes because God is still powerfully working in His world. And love always perseveres. It never fails. We just keep loving and loving and loving, no matter what, because we are linked to the infinitely loving Lover.

NURTURING INTIMACY—THE PATH TO LOVE

How do we get this love operating in our lives? It is a gift from God and the gift of God Himself living in us. God does not give us love so much as He gives us Himself. He lives and loves in and through us. "The springs of love are in God, not in us. It is absurd to look for the love of God in our hearts naturally, it is only there when it has been shed abroad in our hearts by the Holy Spirit," wrote Oswald Chambers.

The Holy Spirit who lives in us grows in us "the fruit of the spirit . . . love" (Gal. 5:22). We give ourselves to Him and grant Him freedom to love through us. We can express this in a simple prayer: "Father, love that person through me. I want to be a conduit of Your love. Show me what that means in practical acts and words." Then we wait patiently to see love blossom, form the first green, hard berries, and go on to mature into ripening fruit. Staying yielded to His will, we grow in love that crowds out selfishness, rudeness, impatience, fear, apathy, and resentment.

We make the conditions conducive for that growth by nurturing intimacy with God. The more we get to know Him and ourselves and integrate that understanding in a way that changes us, the more we will experience and then express His agape. We will never give what we don't have ourselves. As the old farmer said, "You can't give what you ain't got, any more than you can come back from where you ain't been." So the extent to which we understand and appropriate our Father's love for us is the degree to which we can love others. Our love for people will always be the overflow of the fullness of our own love relationship with our heavenly Husband, Parent, Friend.

Here's the promise of what we can be as we draw close to Jesus Christ, a promise of what we may hope to experience and express in our relationships:

> As God's chosen people, holy and dearly loved, clothe yourselves with compassion, kindness, humility, gentleness and patience. Bear with each other and forgive whatever grievances you may have against one another. Forgive as the Lord forgave you. And over all these virtues put on love, which binds them all together in perfect unity.
>
> Let the peace of Christ rule in your hearts, since as members of one body you were called to peace. And be thankful. Let the word of Christ dwell in you richly as

you teach and admonish one another with
all wisdom, and as you sing psalms, hymns
and spiritual songs with gratitude in your
hearts to God. And whatever you do, whether
in word or deed, do it all in the name of the
Lord Jesus, giving thanks to God the Father
through him (Col. 3:12–17, NIV).

In short, we will become like our loving Friend,
and that will be our witness.

"All the world loves a lover," as the saying
goes. That may be a bit of an overstatement,
but there's some validity to the idea. Love isn't
easy to resist; it usually creates a positive response.
As Augustine put it, "One loving heart sets another on fire." Generally, the loving God who
is resident in us attracts people to Himself through
us.

And that's exactly what we desire because
the nature of love is to want everybody to love
our beloved. I want my parents to love my husband, my husband to love my friends, my friends
to love my children. Likewise, we who know
and love God want to help others come to love
Him also. We do that by letting His love in our
lives spill over to them. That's what witness is
all about.

And those who respond to that love won't
all look alike. Just as no two earthly friendships
are the same, so each of us has a unique relationship to the Lord. Each Christian's individuality

will be reflected in his or her walk with and witness to the Lord. That's why we must allow God to be original in our spiritual lives and in the lives of those we seek to make disciples. While all of us believers subscribe to a body of commonly held doctrines and biblical principals, our Teacher personally tailors the curriculum to each pupil's needs. So when we look at God's intimates, we'll discover that no one person's experience is normative for everybody else.

As Emmanual Suhard wrote, "To be a witness does not consist of engaging in propaganda . . . it means living our lives in such a way that one's life would not make sense if God did not exist." To live in such a way that folks see our good deeds and glorify our Abba in heaven is the result of drawing near Him so that we, His intimates, become like Him in love and righteousness, grace and truth.

CHAPTER 14

HURDLE THE BARRIERS

Sarah and Garry married because they wanted to spend the rest of their lives together. Later, they divorced because they saw wedlock as a life sentence. Between those two events, they experienced increasing disconnectedness. Along the way they found themselves confronted, as all married people are, with choices about revealing their deep-down selves to each other, communicating honestly, accepting each other as they are, trusting each other. They decided the challenge of that kind of intimacy was too threatening, too risky. So they opted for being married singles for a while—living together with little spirit or soul intimacy. This ultimately led to their becoming single singles.

That seems to describe the way some relate to their heavenly Bridegroom. They make an initial commitment to accept Him into their lives, but along the line they back away from deepening their union with Him. They don't develop the immensely satisfying relationship with the Lover of their souls that brings them joy, peace, communion, strength, fulfillment, security, and a sense of belonging, being valued and cared for by Him. The good news is that, in spite of this, God doesn't see divorcing them as an option.

BARRIERS TO INTIMACY

What, specifically, keeps you from nurturing intimacy with God? As you've read the previous chapters, what have been your points of tension about engaging in this venture? The reasons probably differ from person to person. A man may wonder if the Lord will ask him to give up his pursuit of financial success. A woman who loves her job may fear that growing in faith will require her to live out a traditional female role that would in some way interfere with her climb up the professional ladder.

Some fear that in drawing close to Jesus they'll be asked to forgive a person who has grievously hurt them, and they can't imagine doing that. Spouses may resist connecting too closely

with God and doing His will because they suspect
that will mean loving each other unselfishly as
Christ loves them. And that kind of love, they
fear, would make them too vulnerable to being
taken for granted or too open to the pain of
rejection.

My own wrestling in this area took a couple of strange turns. For one, some had insinuated
to me that the life of faith required intellectual
suicide. I wondered if closely following Christ
meant putting my brain in cold storage, and that
certainly didn't appeal to me. I had also met up
with my share of rigidly pious types whom I
considered totally unappealing. They dressed
funny and their lives and conversations seemed
irrelevant to me. I questioned whether God
would make me become as odd and unattractive
to other people as those religious models were
to me. I also dealt long and hard with the idea
that to walk closely with Jesus could create distance between me and the people I cared about.
Would they find my relationship with my heavenly Father a barrier to our friendship?

The latter was of special concern to me
in regard to Lowell. I had known Christ for thirteen years when I began to date him, and he
had known Him only a year. I seriously considered the possibility of not pursuing Christ with
more energy than he did. (How I could judge
his fervency is unclear to me now—chock it up
to my immaturity.) I even thought of putting

my spiritual life on hold for a while to lessen the distance between us. I had been confused by some erroneous teaching I'd heard about my husband's being my leader in spiritual things. Thus, I wondered if it was my obligation to leave room for his leading by purposefully limiting my spiritual growth until he was far out in front of me in his knowledge and experience of the Word. Though that concept seems absolutely ridiculous to me now, I assure you I sincerely considered it back then. And I wish I had a quarter for every woman who has expressed the same idea to me over the years. (If this notion were valid, then a Christian woman married to an unbeliever couldn't grow spiritually.)

So when we think about nurturing intimacy with God, we need to confront certain questions: Do I want this? With all my heart? Unconditionally? Irrevocably? What are those things that keep us from a commitment to know Him and ourselves and then integrate our knowledge so that it makes us more like our Father?

Maybe the answers we find within us point out an ambivalence: We want it; we don't want it. We're afraid we won't achieve it; we're scared we'll be disappointed if we do. We wonder if we can handle the risk of change inherent in having an increasingly vital relationship with the Lord. On the other hand, we doubt we can tolerate *not* growing in the grace and knowledge of Jesus Christ. What if we don't think the benefits of intimacy are worth the effort of drawing near to Him?

Doubt

Perhaps some of us are still struggling with doubt. We aren't convinced we can have a warm, satisfying relationship with God. As we discussed in previous chapters, some feel so insignificant or inadequate they have a hard time believing God even cares about being close to them. As one man told me, "I see myself way out on the edge of the crowd that surrounds Jesus. I'm just glad I'm in the crowd at all. I can't imagine that I will be allowed or encouraged to get any closer to Him."

This man had experienced esteem-destroying relationships, so it's not hard to understand why he had a difficult time accepting that "he who comes to God must believe that He is, and that *He is a rewarder of those who diligently seek Him*" (Heb. 11:6, italics mine). Yet He is the God who never casts out or drives away those who come to Him (John 6:37). He comes near those who draw near to Him (James 4:8).

We need have no misgivings about the fact that God made us to be in relationship with Him. He wants intimacy with us more than we want it with Him. He didn't consider the life of His Son too much of a price to pay to make that possible. We confront our doubts about this with a choice to believe that He is indeed the Husband who seeks out even the adulterous wife and the Father who throws a party for a prodigal child.

Fear

Another barrier we may be wrestling with is fear. Some of us may believe that what we don't know can't hurt us. We sense that getting close to God and being truthful before Him may result in traumatic discoveries about who we really are. Thus, we resist the thought of journaling or developing relationships in koinonia because these will inevitably lead to self-discovery. To opt for honesty can be scary. Our encouragement to risk, as we noted earlier, comes in realizing that the reality of who we are certainly won't shock God since He already knows all about us and loves us anyway.

Maybe our anxiety stems not from what we'll discover but from what we already know, so we oppose koinonia because it may force us to reveal the truth about ourselves to others. Since many of us work hard at putting our best selves forward and hiding our weaknesses, we shy away from letting another close enough to know us as we really are. Though we saw in chapter 9 how friends can radically change our perceptions of ourselves to our benefit, we may become downright panic-stricken about unveiling our souls to brothers and sisters in Christ. As a result, we cling to superficial relationships in order to avoid the embarrassment of exposing our inadequacies and possibly enduring the pain of others' rejection.

We may also fear we will have to give up some cherished misconceptions about God as we grow in our knowledge of Him through the Word and the ministry of the Holy Spirit. I've watched people in my Bible class struggle to accept the declaration of a loving Father that His Son is the *only* way to Him. A couple of them had a hard time committing to the study because they perceived this as rigid. Some of us may want to hold on to an erroneous view of God because we're comfortable with it. We can't imagine a God who is vastly superior to our concept of Him.

In addition to these fears, we may fear that intimacy with God will create its own kind of loneliness. As I indicated a few paragraphs back, this was my concern. Instinctively, if not by experience, I knew that those who determine to run well the course God gives them may find they are not in the pack but racing alone. Perhaps most of us suspect that the journey "is always and inevitably lonely out on the growing edge," as Scott Peck put it.[1] But you and I are called to confront our fear of intimacy by trusting the

God who never forsakes us but walks with us even through the valley of the shadow of death.

Impatience

Impatience is another block to intimacy. To grow a relationship takes time. Getting to know another is a slow, lengthy process that never ends. Bigger biceps or thinner thighs may be possible in thirty days, but not firm, lasting relationships. Likewise, in the spiritual realm there are no overnight successes. Yet this idea is hard to swallow. I know I'd like to think that sometime—and the sooner the better—I'll arrive spiritually. But I won't and neither will you. To meditate, pray, read Scripture, journal, and spend time in fellowship with others and then to change because of what we discover is a lifetime process.

Nurturing intimacy with God requires a commitment to the long haul. If we insist on instant mashed potatoes or instant intimacy, we will never taste the real thing. No wonder, then, the Bible exhorts us to stick-to-itiveness in the crucial issues of life. "Let us run with endurance the race that is set before us" (Heb. 12:1). We must come to grips with the fact that developing a relationship takes time—all our years on earth, to be exact. In the spiritual realm, we realize that God is not in a hurry. "He has made everything beautiful in its time" (Eccl. 3:11). We confront our impatience by reminding ourselves that His timing, and not ours, is the important issue.

Laziness

Another huge obstruction to our intimacy with God may be laziness. Relationships always mean work. Learning, growing, and loving of necessity involve energy. I'm hit forcefully with this fact every time I attend a wedding. Underneath my joy for the bride and groom is the awareness of the gigantic effort Lowell and I have expended in the process of becoming one. I've never worked so hard at anything as I have at my marriage—learning to listen, to keep quiet, to speak up, to comfort, to accept, to forgive, to yield, to stand firm, to trust, and lots more. And I still have a ways to go after twenty-seven years.

I've been a believer in Jesus Christ for more than forty years, and I've a long way to go in that relationship too. That means sometimes I've had to shun the comfortable, convenient, and easy route. I've had to roll up my sleeves and toss out the stuff that gets in the way of my intimacy with Him—laziness, fear, doubt, apathy.

I've discovered, however, that love lightens the task in relationships. As Gordon MacDonald wrote, "Passion—the kind that causes some to excel beyond anyone else—dulls one's sense of fatigue, pain, and the need for pleasure or even well-being."[2] We find a biblical confirmation of this idea in the story of Jacob. He "served seven years for Rachel, and they seemed but only a few days to him because of the love he had for her" (Gen. 29:20). As the boy said as he carried a crippled child, "He ain't heavy, he's my brother." Though relationships may require as much work as cleaning house or clearing my desk, it's a good kind of tiredness, infinitely more rewarding than any other activity.

So when I use the word *work,* I'm not thinking of fist-clenching determination to endure drudgery for a good end, but a love-energized drive to do what's necessary to achieve the goal. Where does that love come from? Our Bridegroom. We love Him because He first loved us. We confront our laziness by asking Him to impart to us the passion to pursue Him.

THE CHOICE IS OURS

I could mention other things that get in the way of intimacy—wrong priorities, guilt, anger at God for not jumping through our hoops, love of a secret sin. You may have your own reasons to add to that list. Perhaps, however, the ultimate barrier for any of us is lack of will.

Some of us don't want to be close to God, to be whole. When Jesus approached the crippled man written of in John 5, He asked, "Do you want to be well and whole?" When I first read that, I thought, *What kind of a question is that to ask a person who's been significantly immobile for thirty-eight years? Shouldn't Jesus have assumed the man would say yes?* As I've pondered this, it's dawned on me that He should not have expected a positive response.

Illogical or insane as it may seem, we don't always want what's best for us. Even we who believe in Jesus are notorious for making hurtful choices. That's why many actively or (more likely) passively decide to take the path leading to spiritual mediocrity or worse.

We must understand that nurturing intimacy with God requires a choice, a commitment. It never just happens any more than a great marriage just happens or excellent parenting just happens or significant friendships just happen. Intimacy requires that we deliberately determine that we want it above all else. We will be as whole or as holy as we choose to be.

Perhaps the failure to decide not to dedicate ourselves wholeheartedly to nurture intimacy with God is because we don't believe it's the pearl worth possessing at any cost (Matt. 13:45–46). If we don't think that, what can we do about it? Pray and trust that God will work in us to help us to put Him and His righteousness above all. We pray that He will give us Paul's fervent conviction: "I consider everything a loss compared to the surpassing greatness of knowing

Christ Jesus my Lord. . . . I want to know Christ. . . . I press on to take hold of that for which Christ Jesus took hold of me. . . . All of us who are mature should take such a view of things" (Phil. 3:8–15, NIV).

Lord, we want to be whole. Help us take the mature view of the value of our relationship with You. Create in us a hunger and thirst to know You more than anyone or anything else in the world. Give us a consuming passion to draw near to You. Enable us to embrace this process joyfully, expectantly, until the day when You, our Bridegroom, welcome us home.

NOTES

CHAPTER ONE

1. Walter Wangerin, *As for Me and My House* (Nashville, TN: Thomas Nelson Publishers, 1987), 57.
2. Paul Tillich, *The Eternal Now* (New York: Scribner, 1963), 15–16.

CHAPTER TWO

1. Harold Bloomfield, *Making Peace With Your Parents* (New York: Ballantine Books, 1983), 10, 12.
2. Hannah Whitall Smith, *The God of All Comfort* (Chicago: Moody Press, 1956), 67.
3. Matthew 5:16, 45, 48; 6:1–8, 14–18, 26–34; 7:11.
4. Smith, *The God of All Comfort,* 70.

CHAPTER THREE

1. C. S. Lewis, *The Four Loves* (New York: Harcourt Brace Jovanovich, Inc., 1960), 148.

CHAPTER FOUR

1. Kenneth Swanson, *Uncommon Prayer* (New York: A Ballantine/Epiphany Book, 1987), 52.
2. Joni Eareckson Tada, *Secret Strength* (Portland, OR: Multnomah Press, 1988), 163.
3. J. I. Packer, *Knowing God* (Downers Grove, IL: Inter-Varsity Press, 1973), 36.

4. Ibid., 41.

5. David Seamands, *Healing Grace* (Wheaton, IL: Victor Books, 1988), 28.

6. Source: *Strong's Exhaustive Concordance of the Bible* and *Vine's Expository Dictionary of New Testament Words*. Some versions translate *sophronismos,* self-discipline or self-control, but others use sound mind in passages such as in 2 Timothy 1:7. Various versions translate words in Mark 5:15, 2 Corinthians 5:13, and 1 Timothy 3:2 deriving from the same root as: "in his/our right mind" and "sober minded."

All this indicates to me that true spiritual discipline is a matter of thinking seriously, assessing correctly, and rationally determining our appropriate response to God under the guidance of Scripture and the Spirit. Thus, our spiritual exercises originate in our mind and will, which are directed and energized by the Holy Spirit. In a real sense, then, this is not *self*-discipline (drummed up by us) but *Spirit*-control motivating us. As a result, even a naturally undisciplined person may express the fruit of the Spirit which is temperance or self-control, as some versions translate it (Gal. 5:23).

7. Hannah Whitall Smith, *The Christian's Secret of a Happy Life* (Westwood, NJ: Fleming H. Revell Company, 1952), 27.

8. Fearing God, as Scripture commands, has to do with reverential awe. He wants us to respect Him for who and what He is, not be scared to death of Him.

9. John Piper, *Desiring God* (Portland, OR: Multnomah Press, 1986), 77.

10. Paul Tournier, *Escape from Loneliness* (Philadelphia, PA: Westminster Press, 1962), 114.

CHAPTER FIVE

1. A. W. Tozer, *The Knowledge of the Holy* (Harrisburg, PA: Christian Publications, Inc., 1961), 9–12.

CHAPTER SIX

1. Packer, *Knowing God*, 31.

CHAPTER EIGHT

1. Clifford Williams, "When Mercy Hurts," *Christianity Today*, 3 Feb. 1989, 16.
2. Williams, "When Mercy Hurts," 16–17.
3. This concept of self is not original with me, but I cannot pinpoint the source.
4. Packer, *Knowing God*, 37.
5. Williams, "When Mercy Hurts," 17.
6. Wangerin, *As for Me and My House*, 58.
7. Seamands, *Healing Grace*, 180.
8. James M. Houston, "The Independence Myth," *Christianity Today*, 15 Jan. 1990, 32–33.
9. Thomas a Kempis, *The Imitation of Christ* (Chicago, IL: Moody Press), 16.

CHAPTER NINE

1. Watchman Nee, *A Table in the Wilderness* (Fort Washington, PA: Christian Literature Crusade, 1971), 20.
2. Harry J. Cargas and Rojer J. Radley, *Keeping a Spiritual Journal* (Garden City, NJ: Doubleday, 1981), 8.
3. Morton Kelsey, *Adventure Inward* (Minneapolis: Augsburg Fortress, 1980).
4. Richard Foster, *Freedom of Simplicity*, (San Francisco, CA: Harper & Row, 1979), 47.
5. Kelsey, *Adventure Inward*.
6. David McKenna, "That Amazing Grace," *Christianity Today*, 13 May 1988, 22.

CHAPTER TEN

1. Richard Foster, *The Celebration of Discipline* (San Francisco, CA: Harper & Row, 1988), 20–21.

2. Packer, *Knowing God*, 18–19.
3. Foster, *The Celebration of Discipline*, 21.

CHAPTER ELEVEN

1. Oswald Chambers, *My Utmost for His Highest* (New York: Dodd, Mead & Company, 1965), 88.
2. Ibid., 129.
3. Andrew Murray, *Like Christ* (New York: Grosset & Dunlap), 119.

CHAPTER TWELVE

1. Swanson, *Uncommon Prayer*, 46.
2. Murray, *Like Christ*, 108.
3. Edward Le Joly, *Mother Teresa of Calcutta* (San Francisco: Harper & Row, Publishers, 1983), 213.
4. Murray, *Like Christ*, 109.
5. C. S. Lewis, *Letters to Malcolm* (New York: Harcourt, Brace & World, Inc., 1963), 82.

CHAPTER THIRTEEN

1. Nicolas Wolterstorff in *The Reformed Journal* as quoted in *Christianity Today*, 7 August 1987.
2. Henry Drummond, *The Greatest Thing in the World* (Old Tappan, NJ: Fleming H. Revell Co., 1970), 13–14.
3. This should in *no* way be interpreted to mean that to passively accept injury to our bodies or psyches is virtuous. Love will not allow another to demean and disgrace himself by abusing others, including ourselves.

CHAPTER FOURTEEN

1. Scott Peck, *The Road Less Traveled* (New York: Simon and Schuster, 1987), 168.
2. Gordon MacDonald, *Restoring Your Spiritual Passion* (Nashville, TN: Oliver-Nelson, 1986), 18.